THE
SEVEN SECRETS OF SUCCESSFUL AUTHORS

A Proven System for Writing a Strategic Book That Avoids Costly Mistakes and Creates More Profit!

Kevin Bermingham

www.TheSuccessfulAuthor.com

The Seven Secrets of Successful Authors

First published in Great Britain in 2012

Second edition, 2013.

Published by The Successful Author, an imprint of Meaningful Goals Ltd., Sussex, England. www.TheSuccessfulAuthor.com

Author's photograph © 2013 by John Cassidy

A catalogue record for this book is available from the British Library.

Digital Edition	ISBN 978-1-908101-75-4
Paperback Edition	ISBN 978-1-908101-74-7

PRAISE FOR

The Seven Secrets of Successful Authors
A Proven System for Writing a Strategic Book That
Avoids Costly Mistakes and Creates More Profit!
by Kevin Bermingham

"For me, the most important part of this book was when I worked out who my reader was in detail. I'd had a rough idea and a lot of passion that I wanted to get my message 'out there' but no more than that. The process of getting inside my perfect reader's head was really useful and it made such a difference to my ability to focus as I wrote my book. If I later got lost and started to waffle, then I just went back to my perfect reader's profile and refocused myself to write for that person. Very helpful. And now, it's amazing that the 'perfect reader' that I wrote my book for is exactly the person who now buys my published book. And they even write brilliant book reviews for me on Amazon, because my book 'hit the spot' for them."

Helen Turier RGN MAR
Resilience and Wellbeing Practitioner, trainer, and author of four books:
Bounce-back Ability, Get Back on Your Feet Again, Managing Pressure and Change Effectively, and *Discover How Your Lifestyle Could be Killing You*
www.helenturier.com

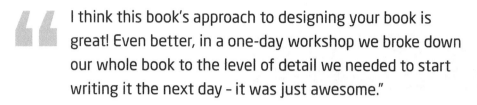

"I think this book's approach to designing your book is great! Even better, in a one-day workshop we broke down our whole book to the level of detail we needed to start writing it the next day – it was just awesome."

Alun Richards
Author of two books: *The Seven Critical Website Mistakes* and *Fire Your Webmaster*
www.yourwebmasterisfired.co.uk

"Kevin has developed a simple strategy to get your ideas organised, your writing done, your deliveries scheduled, and he even guarantees that you'll hold your published book in your hand within 90 days."

Martin Cornes
Author of three books: *The Ultimate Profit System, The Seven Killer Business Mistakes* and *Why Personal Development Doesn't Work*
www.theultimateprofitsystem.co.uk

"Kevin has created a fine-tuned strategy that takes the hard work out of writing a book for all would-be authors. It takes dedication and commitment from an author and with Kevin's fool proof plan to follow; you're well on the road to success, while keeping your sanity!"

Elaine Noble
Certified life coach and author of *Everyday Mistakes That Undermine Your Confidence*
www.mistakesthatundermineyourconfidence.co.uk

I think people experience a surge of overwhelm when they consider everything that's involved in writing a book. So I would say the biggest secret for me was simply the fact that one can design a whole book in a day! Yes, that is definitely the biggest thing that I took away. I remember thinking – WHAT? Are you crazy? One day to design my book and then I will be completely ready to write it? But I was … and I did! It was nothing short of remarkable. Thank you Kevin!"

Jennie Harland-Khan
Mentor, speaker and author of *I'm BACK! How to get your passion, purpose and identity back when your kids go to school*
www.jenniehk.com

I attended a ministerial event earlier in the week and all I did was tell some important person that I had just written a book and what the book was about. Now I've just been offered an opportunity to undertake a professional doctorate. The moral is, tell everyone you meet – whether they appear interested or not. You never know who they are or who they know. I'm getting this scary feeling that my book is going to open some doors. So I must get ready to handle what it brings with it! It felt right, from the word go. I can smell the aroma of sweet success."

Ruth Tosin Oshikanlu RN (Adult), RM, RSCPHN (Health Visiting), QN
Midwife and health visitor and author of: *Tune In To Your Baby: Because babies don't come with an instruction manual*
www.tuneintoyourbaby.co.uk

Writing my book has been a 'dream come true.' If anyone had asked me if I could write a book 90 days ago, the answer would have been questionable. I never believed I could, but I have! The amazing feeling of holding my completed book in my hand after 90 days – and then selling it – is something special to experience. Thank you, my book mentor and publisher; your inspiration and encouragement have been awesome. I'd recommend you and your 90-day programme to anyone – because we all have a book in us!"

Lynn Tulip Chartered MCIPD
Independent career consultant, counsellor and HR professional. Author of two books: *Get That Job: The art of successful job hunting* and *Can't Get That Job: Seven killer CV mistakes that destroy your chances of job success*
www.getthatjobbook.com

Also by

Kevin Bermingham

Change Your Limiting Beliefs:
Three Steps to Achieve Meaningful Goals

www.ChangeYourLimitingBeliefs.co.uk

"
Change Your Limiting Beliefs has a clear message – we can change our beliefs for the better and make them suit the lives we want as individuals. It makes sense; I understood it all and it's in a logical sequence. The exercises work; they 'fit' into the overall structure and are applicable to my style of learning. Did I find it useful and relevant? Totally!"

Martin Cornes
Director, The Coaching Foundation Ltd, 2012.

CONTENTS

ACKNOWLEDGEMENTS

Firstly, I'd like to acknowledge the inspiration I received from Rudyard Kipling (1865-1936), whose poem from The Elephant's Child[1] has provided the framework upon which I've build The Seven Secrets of Successful Authors and planned the majority of my lifetime's projects.

I would also like to acknowledge those from whom I've learned so much. Their insights have influences much within these pages. In no particular order: Christopher Howard, Dr. Joanna Martin, Daniel Wagner, Daniel Priestley, Dan Bradbury, Peter Thomson, Mike Harris, Robert Cialdini, Dan Poynter and Brian Tracey.

I'd also like to acknowledge the lessons received from those authors who have been clients of mine; some of whose work is illustrated on the next page. Each one of you taught me so much without knowing it. I applaud you all for diligently following the advice that's now contained within The Seven Secrets of Successful Authors and for getting a Strategic Book out of your head and into your hands within just 90 days. Congratulations!

---

1   Just-So Stories, 1902 (publ. Macmillan & Co.)

www.TheSuccessfulAuthor.com

FOREWORD
by DANIEL WAGNER

I met Kevin Bermingham only a few months ago. He attended a discovery day at our head office in Wokingham and he stood out from the crowd by persistently asking detailed questions.

I quickly learned that Kevin had been successful in many areas of his life, which is great, because I believe that if you have managed to achieve success in any field, you possess the qualities and mind-set to transfer that skill-set to other areas.

When Kevin told me that he helps authors become successful by writing a *Strategic Book* using a formula, I was delighted. It is one of the key pieces of the puzzle to help experts achieve public recognition, and I really wanted him to become part of my Expert Success Academy.

Kevin soon joined the Expert Success Academy and we decided to embark on our first publishing project together. *Expert Success Stories* is a book comprising chapters from 29 different contributors. The project's success was largely a result of Kevin's dedication and ability to help people get results fast! He has not just proven himself capable; he has shown tremendous tact and skill in pulling together and managing the work of so many people in an impossibly short period.

Through his publishing services, Kevin will help many of our Academy members to increase both their self-belief and their positioning as authorities in the marketplace. His generous contributions and support for the Expert Success Academy family makes him a much loved and appreciated member.

So this is my way of saying thank you to Kevin Bermingham, the project manager of my book. I found him to be trustworthy, responsible and extremely efficient in his ability to getting things done. Kevin, I couldn't have done it without you.

Daniel Wagner, Expert Success LLP

www.expertsuccessformula.com

19 June 2013

INTRODUCTION

I believe the very best way to attract pre-sold prospects for your business, whilst simultaneously raising your personal profile head and shoulders above your competitors, is by writing a STRATEGIC BOOK - *if it's done right!*

Kevin Bermingham

Few authors make money from book sales; so don't waste time writing a self-indulgent book you'll never sell - write a strategic book instead.

The Seven Secrets of Successful Authors is the first step towards planning, publishing, and productising your strategic book correctly, so that it becomes a laser-focussed marketing tool that gives you more clarity, credibility, and collateral.

When helping business owners, entrepreneurs and specialists to become successful authors, I use a proven three-step formula, supported by a foolproof project plan, so they get it all done quickly and avoid costly mistakes.

- Plan to **achieve strategic clarity**
- Publish to **boost personal credibility**
- Productise to **create profitable collateral**

A strategic book acts like a brochure or business card on steroids. So don't waste time selling your book, let your book sell you!

As a publisher and authors' mentor, I'm known for helping business owners, entrepreneurs and specialists to write what I call a 'strategic book' that gives them more clarity, credibility and collateral, than their competitors.

While every aspiring author has their own reason for wanting to write a book, the sad fact is that the majority don't succeed. And those that do manage to write it may find their manuscript just languishes in their bottom drawer, never to take life in print. Perhaps that's the saddest outcome of all.

I frequently meet people who say they want to write a book, but can't. So often, they started off with high hopes, but somehow lost their way as time went on.

Me 'What are you doing these days?'

Aspiring author 'I'm writing a book.'

Me 'Really? How long have you been doing that?'

Aspiring author 'Er, a couple of years now ... but I've finally got it sorted and I know where I'm going with it now ... and ... well, anyway, things just get in the way, don't they ... and, well, you just know when it's the right time ... don't you?'

Yes, it's an all too familiar story, isn't it?

We've all met someone like this and, if we're sensible, we change the subject, before our own spirits get dragged down too. It doesn't have to be like this; although everyone is different.

So how can you, an aspiring author, avoid making the same costly mistakes and avoid failure or disappointment?

You see, there are many reasons why the **DREAMERS** don't even start their books. And equally, there are many reasons why other people do start but often don't finish. Some people are **EAGER** to start, but just don't know how or where. While others are inspired and motivated enough to put pen to paper, yet somehow they got **STUCK**; they got **LOST** along the way and don't quite know why. Well, the good news is that it's not their fault! So, which type of author are you?

- **Dreamer**
- **Eager**
- **Stuck**
- **Lost**
- **Published**

Would you be surprised to know that, whatever type of author you are now, there's a simple, foolproof system for writing a book - with every step already planned and mapped out in detail for you - that you can easily follow in order to become better?

That's right: in this book, you will follow an easy, step-by-step process to create a sure-fire book proposal that will get your expertise out of your head and into print sooner than you ever imagined possible, so that you quickly become a successful author.

I was a successful project manager and management consultant for over twenty years and in that time discovered how to get things done on time, when others couldn't. I've since moved on to become a book publisher and authors' mentor. And, incredible though it seems, I still use those same project-management techniques, but now I help authors to get their books written and published – FAST!

I mainly work one-to-one with aspiring authors to help them create a strategic plan for their book - so they write the 'Right Book' - and continue to provide ongoing consultancy services to assure its each book's success. I also provide group programmes, which reduce the cost of my time without compromising on results.

'It's often said that "We've all got a book within us." And if you've ever questioned the validity of that statement, then you need to meet Kevin Bermingham. Kevin has developed a simple strategy to get your ideas organised, your writing done, your deliveries scheduled, and then he'll ensure you'll actually hold your published book in your hand - all within 90 days. If you think that sounds incredible, there's more. Because along the way, Kevin coaches and mentors you; providing a complete service that's truly amazing. In my case, after starting off really well, I found myself facing several major, technical and domestic challenges along the way. But Kevin's positive approach, support, and guidance ensured I still finished what I'd started, and all within the 90 days. I can highly recommend this first-class, 90-day programme. It easily proves the truth that "We've all got a book within us".'

Martin Cornes
Author of three books: *The Ultimate Profit System, The Seven Killer Business Mistakes* and *Why Personal Development Doesn't Work*
www.theultimateprofitsystem.co.uk

In fact, if someone joins my group-mentoring programme, I'll guarantee that, if they work diligently, I can get their book out of their head and into their hands within 90 days, or I'll give their money back.

Over the years, I've spent a lot of time looking back over my time as a project manager to identify the essential keys to success. You see, the secret of my success came from avoiding the same old dumb mistakes that came up time after time; then I found that the same old dumb mistakes were being made by authors too. Of course, writing a book is also a project, so I applied the very same solutions I'd used as a corporate project manager and found that they also worked for me as an author.

Although I dress up these solutions as secrets, in reality they're just simple, but effective, systems-analysis and project-management techniques that I have discovered. And they will work for you! I know, because I've already tested them extensively.

Some people spend two to three years writing a book, but don't despair - there is an alternative. You see, not many people have that amount of time available, so I designed my programme to include no more than eight weeks of writing.

However, to be successful, you'll need to work within Pareto's principle, known as the 80:20 rule. By that, I mean that you can always complete 80 per cent of any task in just 20 per cent of the time it would take to complete the full 100 per cent. To put it another way, the last 20 per cent of any task consumes 80 per cent of the effort. I always encourage authors to accept that a score of 8/10 for their book will be perfectly adequate for them and their readers. Otherwise, they will spend at least 18 months writing and 'polishing', their manuscript and then a further 18 months getting it published – and life's too short for that!

'Every publishing house, large or small, is bombarded all day every day with would-be authors, striving to get the publisher to look at their manuscript. Publishers throw them in the trash without reading them. The key to get a hearing with a literary agent, and then later with a publisher, is a BOOK PROPOSAL.'

Brian Tracy
Bestselling author

Even better, there's no need to spend time on research – you'll get by with what you already know. You see, you can't become an expert if you write about things you've had to look up first. So just write what you already know, in your own words, and your credibility will be enhanced because you can later talk about any aspect of your book's contents without needing to go find the statistics and figures you researched to write the book. What people really value is your 'take' on the subject; that's what makes you different. It's your opinion that makes you the expert!

Here are some common myths that often hold back aspiring authors.

Some Common Myths

Lack of experience

> *'I have a lot of experience in my field of expertise, but I certainly couldn't write an entire book about it.'*

Writing a book is easier than you think. If you follow the system outlined in this book, you will write a book proposal that will easily demonstrate that you have more than enough material to write a book. Of course, you could just choose to publish your book in a smaller format. For example, a pocket-sized book, which could be given away for marketing purposes, need have only 72 or 80 pages in order to have a proper spine with its title printed on it. It need be only 7,000–15,000 words long and could easily be written in a week or even a weekend.

I don't have time

> *'I don't have time to sit down and write a book. Doesn't it take years?'*

Well, first of all, I'd like to remind you that you have 24 hours a day, seven days a week, just like every other published author on the planet. As for it taking years, I've found that, with a good design and my foolproof plan, anyone can finish a manuscript for a 200-page book in just 90 minutes a day, over eight weeks. Then my editing, publishing and printing process increases the total time to 90 days.

Years indeed, bah!

People won't want it

> *'I've often fantasised about writing a book. I have the material, but I'm not sure how to write something that people will pay for.'*

Good point! Why don't you ask them before you start? I recommend that you first write a book proposal. Not only does this ensure that you avoid common mistakes, but it addresses any uncertainties about WHO to write for (see Chapter 2). You see, successful authors don't write a book and then wait to see if anybody wants it. Instead, they decide exactly who needs their information, so that they know those people will want to read it.

It won't get published

> *'Maybe I could write an entire book, but how would I get it published?'*

We're lucky these days. Never in the whole of human history has it been easier for ordinary people to become published authors. In fact, there are three publishing strategies you could choose from:

1. **Traditional publishing strategy.** For those who want to "sell" their book. Good, if you have a large following of people who are eager to buy your book.

2. **Self-publishing strategy.** Not for the technically challenged, nor those short of time.

Most book marketing today is done by authors, not by publishers. Publishers have managed to stay afloat in this worsening marketplace only by shifting more and more marketing responsibility to authors, to cut costs and prop up sales. In recognition of this reality, most book proposals from experienced authors now have an extensive (usually many pages) section on the authors' marketing platform and what the authors will do to publicize and market the books. Publishers still fulfil important roles in helping craft books to succeed and making books available in sales channels, but whether the books move in those channels depends primarily on the authors.

Steven Piersanti
President, Berrett-Koehler Publishers. March 6, 2012 [2]

3. **Strategic book approach.** For those who want more clarity, credibility and collateral. Ideal for authors that don't want to 'sell a book', but want a book to 'sell them' instead.

Traditional Publishing Strategy

This strategy is what everyone thinks of, when they consider writing and publishing a book. Somewhat cynically, I call this the *Do-It-Yourself* route. You see, even if you follow the guidance in

---

2 Source: http://www.bkpextranet.com/AuthorMaterials/10AwfulTruths.htm

this book and write a book proposal that avoids all the mistakes of unsuccessful authors, there's still no guarantee that someone will take it off your hands and turn it into an overnight success.

These days, traditional publishers are under great financial pressure. In a world moving away from printed books, **they no longer have the funds to print tens of thousands of books before promoting an unknown author** - that's you!

> The LA Times receives 600 to 700 books for review each week.
>
> **Steve Wasserman,**
> book review editor.[3]

This means that to be published by a traditional publishing house, then you'll need to do a lot of the work. You'll need to plan your book, write it and find a publisher who wants you; then you'll need to have acquired a massive 'social following', on Twitter and Facebook for example, who are eager to buy your book just as soon as it hits the shelves. Even then, you must be prepared to do the majority of the ongoing book promotion yourself.

---

3   Source: http://www.latimes.com

> A larger publisher must sell 10,000 books to break even.
>
> **Brian DeFiore,**
> Maui Writers Conference.[4]

As for author's royalties: you'll be lucky to get £1-2 per copy sold, and most of that will go to repay any author's advance payment you might have received from the publisher (as if!).

Then there's the issue of 'publishing rights'. Will a mainstream publisher want the exclusive rights to your book? Of course they will. That restricts your ability to create videos and training materials based on your own work! I know one author who wanted a PDF copy of the first chapter of his book, so that he could use it as a free promotional 'taster' to be downloaded from his website, but was refused!

Self-Publishing Strategy

These days, it has become much easier for ordinary people to become published authors, because of the advances in printing technology. There are book printing technologies available now that can economically produce batches of bookshop-quality books in very small quantities, sometimes of as few as 100 copies - or fewer, if you're prepared to pay more per copy.

---

4   Source: http://www.parapublishing.com/sites/para/resources/statistics.cfm

For example, I offer some of my more able clients a *Do-It-With-You* self-publishing programme, during which I coach them through the planning, production, and pre-publishing process. Then they set themselves up as publishers and do the rest themselves. However, I can also provide a premium self-publishing service that also sets them up as a self-publisher.

Overall, the advantage of the self-publishing route is that you're not at the mercy of a publisher who has other priorities - you keep all the publishing rights. But this route certainly isn't for the faint-hearted, who might be technically unskilled or short of the extensive amount of time needed to handle the publishing set-up and ongoing administration workload.

> A book has less than a one per cent chance of being stocked in an average bookstore. For every available bookstore shelf space, there are 100 to 1,000 or more titles competing for that shelf space. For example, the number of business titles stocked ranges from less than 100 (smaller bookstores) to approximately 1,500 (superstores). Yet there are 250,000-plus business books in print that are fighting for that limited shelf space.
>
> **Steven Piersanti,**
> President, Berrett-Koehler Publishers. March 6, 2012 [5]

---

5   Source: http://www.bkpextranet.com/AuthorMaterials/10AwfulTruths.htm

The other drawback of self-publishing is that, with a proliferation of mainstream books available, bookshops are reluctant to stock a book from such a publisher, due to their poor quality.

Strategic Book Strategy

Alternatively, there is an innovative strategy open to those who don't need to make money from selling books.

Bowker reports that over three million books were published in the USA in 2010

(May 18, 2011, Bowker Report).

With competition like this, many authors chose not to chase after mainstream publishers. They simply don't need to 'sell their soul' to create a bestseller; but simply wish to write and publish a book that enhances their personal credibility or promotes their business to prospective clients or customers.

And they certainly don't want the hassle of self-publishing!

Strategic Book Formula

Achieve **Strategic Clarity.** Planning a clear strategic direction gives focus.

Boost **Personal Credibility.** Publishing a credible book enhances your personal profile.

Create **Profitable Collateral.** Productising creates profit from your existing skills and knowledge and collateral creates pre-sold prospects who want to become customers.

This strategy differs from the old 'vanity publishing' route where authors paid publishers to publish and print tens of thousands of books - where no demand existed. This route was taken simply to boost the author's ego in the eyes of friends and family. To avoid this type route, I suggest you avoid any publisher who offers you a service that includes the phrase 'bestseller'.

Using my Strategic Book Formula, authors publish their book as an innovative marketing tool.

They don't aim to be rewarded financially from royalties on the book; they want to stand out from the crowd by achieving more **clarity**, **credibility** and **collateral** for themselves and their business.

To support business-owners, entrepreneurs and specialists who qualify to benefit from this strategy, I offer a full end-to-end, *Do-It-For-You* planning, publishing and productising programme.

This approach ideal for authors who don't want to spend their time 'selling books', but who want their book to 'sell them' instead.

Rudyard Kipling's Recipe for Writing Exceedingly Good Books

As a publisher, I've found that aspiring authors seldom take the time to address fundamental questions about their proposed books. And, as a result, the majority of aspiring authors never complete their books.

As a project manager, one of the most useful things I ever came across was a little poem by Rudyard Kipling. Along with other project managers, I found that the secret to avoiding disaster was to start by answering his six (not so simple) questions.

I keep six honest serving-men
(They taught me all I knew);
Their names are What and Why and When
And How and Where and Who.

Rudyard Kipling (1865-1936)

In terms of writing a book, I found it was useful to extend the number of questions by adding *WHICH* and then rearranging their order so Kipling's six questions now become my seven:

What and **Who** and **Why** and **How** and
When and **Where** and **Which**?

The seven secrets of successful authors in this book are simply the answers to those seven great questions; each is designed to focus authors on the right things, before they start writing.

Every aspiring author should take the time to answer these questions. They allow an author to write a book in a fraction of the time it would otherwise take. Also, future editors and publishers will just love the resulting focus and clarity of the author's manuscript. Sometimes this is called the '6-W method'.

For those of you paying attention, I'm not cheating; we still count the HOW, even though its 'W' comes at the end the word!

Personally, I call it Rudyard Kipling's Recipe for Writing Exceedingly Good Books, because I use his six ingredients (plus one of my own) and they always produce a great book.

All my successful authors have diligently followed Mr Kipling's recipe. So, as you read the rest of this book, we'll be following Mr Kipling's (extended) recipe together.

In fact, it's the very same recipe I've always used to plan projects.

The following diagram illustrates the scope of *The Seven Secrets of Successful Authors'* webinar programme, from which this book is written.

The Seven Secrets of Successful Authors

The SEVEN SECRETS of Successful Authors™

A Proven System for PLANNING a Strategic Book That Avoids Costly Mistakes and Creates More Profit!

1. What?	2. Who?	3. Why?	4. How?	5. When?	6. Where?	7. Which?
WHAT to Write About	**WHO to Write For**	**WHY Readers Buy Books**	**HOW to Design Book**	**WHEN to Finish Writing**	**WHERE to Promote Book**	**WHICH Specialists**
MOTIVATING TOPIC	PERFECT READER	YOUR BOOK'S PROMISE	BULLET-PROOF DESIGN	FOOL-PROOF WRITING PLAN	MARKETING PLAN	SUPPORT PLAN
LEARN ABOUT: • Motivating Book Topic: • Problems • Passions • Proficiencies • Book Title • Subtitles	**LEARN ABOUT:** • Choosing For Whom to Write • Demographic Profiles • Perfect Reader: • Names • Situations • Challenges • Objections • Attitudes • Real Quotes • Inside Story	**LEARN ABOUT:** • Psychographic Profiles • Reader's Problems • Author's Solutions • Compelling Sales Copy • Main Themes • Your Book's Promise	**LEARN ABOUT:** • The 3-Book Design Strategy • Book Title • Book Design Disciplines • Book Design Software • Chapter Heads • Sections Heads • Subsections • Cover Design Specification • Marketing Blurb Design • Author Bio.	**LEARN ABOUT:** • Cyclic Writing Strategy • Book Management Software • Author's Work Schedule (Write, Edit & Review) • Publisher's Work Schedule (Design, Edit & Publishing) • Print & Delivery Schedule	**LEARN ABOUT:** • People • Place • Price • Promotion: • Brochure • Flyer • Networking • Website • Download • Articles • Blog Posts • Videos • Seminars • Workshops • Workbooks	**LEARN ABOUT:** • Step-by-Step Programmes • Defined Set of Deliverables • List of Technical Specialists • Coach/Mentors • Project Managers • Accountability • Peer Support Communities • Guaranteed Results

© 2013 K. Bermingham

THE SUCCESSFUL AUTHOR
www.TheSuccessfulAuthor.com

Summary

In this introduction, we've looked at the reasons why you might want to become a published author and what strategies are available. We also explored Rudyard Kipling's (extended) Recipe for Writing Exceedingly Good Books.

This space is for your notes and thoughts.

You should now write some notes and pin them up where you can see them while you're writing your book.

Better still; complete the relevant sections of the Sure-fire Book Proposal Workbook at the end of this chapter or back of the book. As you complete each chapter and learn how to avoid each mistake, you will find that there's a section in the workbook for you to write down your answer. Then they will all be in one place for you to review before doing any writing.

If you'd prefer not to write in the book, you may download a copy of the workbook from:

www.TheSuccessfulAuthor.com/resources

Knowing the secrets of successful authors will help you to avoid the mistakes made by unsuccessful authors. But, clearly, we can't cover everything that you need to know and do within a book. That's why we run group workshops and a series of online webinars. These are designed to walk you through our Sure-fire Book Proposal process. They are designed to drill down into the essential details of your WHAT, WHO, WHY, HOW, WHEN, WHERE, WHICH and provide you with valuable feedback on how you can improve your proposal - and your book.

Remember, it's much faster and easier to refine a book proposal before you start writing your book than it is to rewrite your whole book after it's finished.

If you'd like to discover more about our webinars, workshops or coaching programmes, please visit:

www.TheSuccessfulAuthor.com

SECRET 1

WHAT TO WRITE ABOUT

Secret number one is to know WHAT to write about. This section deals with your motivation and your topic selection.

Some unsuccessful authors may be deterred because they don't know what to write about. Or, if they do, they make the big mistake of starting a book without having a very good, motivating reason for writing it. Most think they'll make money from book sales and they're happy with that motive, so they don't look for a better reason. But if you want to stay sufficiently motivated when things get difficult – and they will – you'll need a much better reason for writing a book.

Successful authors always write on a topic that they're passionate about, knowing that they'll achieve a reward (not necessarily financial), and this motivates them to finish it. You must ensure that there's a hungry market for your book before you write it. But here's the problem: most unsuccessful authors simply assume they'll become famous and successful by making money from book advances or royalties paid by mainstream publishers. And that influences WHAT they decide to write about. But nothing could be further from the truth – unless you're someone like David Attenborough, Nigella Lawson or Paul McKenna, you won't get rich that way!

Here's a blunt fact to consider (you can easily search online for some more statistics, if you want to get really depressed).

'The average book title in America sells about 500 copies.'

Publisher's Weekly [6]

Yes, that's right; just 500 copies sold into a potential US marketplace which is now 314,455,000 people (as of September 2012, the USA is the third most populous country in the world, according to Wikipedia). Assuming an author gets a typical royalty of only £1-2 per copy, one day you're going to decide that it's just not worth bothering to finish writing your book for the expected reward of just £1,000.

Furthermore, the traditional publishing model is available only to those with a proven track record. Traditional, mainstream publishers no longer take on anyone other than the very best, hot prospects. And, even if they do sign up an unknown, they haven't the money or time to promote them. In fact, your book proposal must include a section on how, after publication, you intend to promote and market the book yourself!

Traditional book publishers will get your book into bookshops, but they require you to send readers to the bookshop, otherwise the

---

6   2004. "Of the 950,000 titles out of the 1.2 million tracked by Nielsen Bookscan sold fewer than 99 copies. Another 200,000 sold fewer than 1,000 copies. Only 25,000 sold more than 5,000 copies. The average book in America sells about 500 copies." Publisher's Weekly, July 17, 2006 Source: http://www.parapublishing.com/sites/para/resources/statistics.cfm

book will be withdrawn after a few weeks. Without the industry contacts and financial investment of a mainstream publisher, the prospect of ordinary people making money from book sales is

negligible. It's generally accepted that an expectation of royalties from book sales is no longer a valid reason for writing a book. So if the expectation of making money from publisher's advances and royalties is not a good reason, why else would you write a book?

In my experience, business-owners, entrepreneurs and specialists only become successful authors when they write a Strategic Book. By doing this, they achieve more:

- **CLARITY.** To clarify and focus the author's muddled thinking (that is, to create a more coherent set of ideas that are more easily communicated to others). Sometimes people get by, with no clear sense of purpose or direction. They're incessantly swamped and distracted by competing ideas and conflicting pressures. Their heads are continually in a spin and that means they often suffer from distraction and overwhelm. Writing a book requires laser-like focus, with clear purpose and direction. So, when you've finished your book by focusing on the correct topic and framework, everything becomes so much easier.

- **CREDIBILITY.** Many business-owners, entrepreneurs and specialists are finding business fiercely competitive these days. It's difficult for them to differentiate themselves from their competition, so their prices and fees spiral ever lower. Writing a Strategic Book turns them into experts in their field

- remember, because experts write books, all authors must be experts! And when you're an expert, you don't have any competition. That means you can charge premium prices for your products and services because you are 'the authority' in your field.

- **COLLATERAL.** To create tangible evidence of competence (for example, after readers finish a Strategic Book, they'll often understand the author's business better and may even contact the author having become pre-sold prospects). Most of what we do in our service-based economy is intangible, yet potential customers and clients still look for things they can touch and feel before making a buying decision. A business card and a brochure is really not enough if you want to charge a premium for your services. Handing your published book to a potential client, or emailing them a link to your book's entry on Amazon, provides all the collateral you'll ever need to win more business.

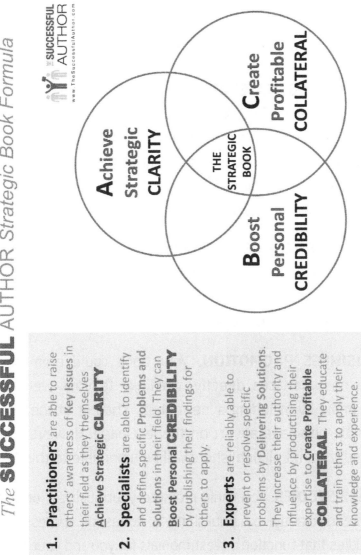

The SUCCESSFUL AUTHOR Strategic Book Formula

1. **Practitioners** are able to raise others' awareness of **Key Issues** in their field as they themselves **Achieve Strategic CLARITY**

2. **Specialists** are able to identify and define specific **Problems and Solutions** in their field. They can **Boost Personal CREDIBILITY** by publishing their findings for others to apply.

3. **Experts** are reliably able to prevent or resolve specific problems by **Delivering Solutions**. They increase their authority and influence by productising their expertise to **Create Profitable COLLATERAL**. They educate and train others to apply their knowledge and experience.

You'll get more Clarity, Credibility and Collateral from publishing a Strategic Book

The Strategic Book Formula

Have you started thinking about your own reasons for writing a book? WHAT you will write about and why? My authors give many reasons for deciding to write a book and their reasons definitely affected their choices of TOPIC.

Here are a few more examples to consider:

- **MARKETING MATERIAL.** You will always have a never-ending source of marketing material for your business. Your book will be a source of coherent extracts that can be re-purposed as articles, blog posts and newsletters; your book will also be a ready-made script for videos and podcasts on the topic about which you've written.

- **SALES BROCHURE.** You could choose to design and write your book as the ultimate sales brochure, or even as just an *industrial-strength business card* that you can hand out at networking meetings or to potential clients.

- **BUSINESS PROMOTION.** Your book could promote your business services directly, via links to your website, for example by including a 'next steps' chapter at the end or a simple one-page advert on the last page. However, bear in mind that not all publishers will be amenable to this.

- **CASE STUDIES.** You could promote your business or services more discreetly, by publishing a series of successful case studies that function as testimonials for you and your business.

- **TRAINING FRAMEWORK.** If your business is based on selling your expertise, your book becomes a powerful framework upon which to build coaching programmes, training courses, sales seminars, webinars and practical workshops.

- **REFERENCE.** To support their internal business processes (for example, this is how we carry on the business of ...).

- **LEGACY.** To leave a legacy (to 'give something back').

- **PUBLICITY.** To get free publicity – becoming an author makes you noteworthy. As one of my authors said:

'I was immediately booked for a radio interview on my topic of Resilience (the ability to bounce back after a setback) as soon as I'd mentioned having published a book on the subject.'

Helen Turier, RGN MAR
Resilience and Wellbeing Practitioner, trainer and author of four books: Bounce-back Ability, Get Back on Your Feet Again, Managing Pressure and Change Effectively, and Discover How Your Lifestyle Could be Killing You
www.helenturier.com

From a practical point of view, if aspiring authors don't know exactly WHAT to write about, then they will have to work out what is their motive for writing the book and then write from that perspective. It's your choice! All successful authors knew their reasons for writing, right from the start.

So how should authors choose between possible topics to write about? How can they choose the one that's best for them?

Sometimes we're tempted to start something without thinking too much about WHY we're doing it, because it just 'feels' right.

To summarise, there are two aspects to your TOPIC that you need to consider:

- Firstly, **MOTIVATION.** If an author's topic isn't important enough to them, they will eventually lose interest and may not even finish, because finishing depends upon motivation!

- Secondly, the **REASON.** Without a topic that provides a compelling reason to write a book, it's difficult to avoid changing topics if we're distracted by other, equally valid ideas. Without a good reason for choosing a topic, an author can get distracted and lose focus. As a result, they may broaden their book's original topic and it may become incoherent, which will confuse their readers. Or else the aspiring author may get overwhelmed by all the options and simply be unable to cope, and then they will give up.

As in every part of life, it's our goals that give us focus and which allow us to recognise distractions for what they are. To ensure that our goals lead us to the results we need, and motivate us along the way, they need to fit within the wider context of factors that are important to us. For authors, if their book doesn't help to support some aspect of their life's purpose in some way, for example by helping them to achieve a goal that they're passionate about, then it simply won't be important enough to maintain their initial motivation and enable them to finish it when things get tough.

Your Book's Topic

Here's a technique that I call 'The Three 'P's of Purpose':

1. Problem
2. Passion
3. Proficiency

I use it to help aspiring authors select their best, most motivating TOPIC.

Let's consider three particular motivators in order to find a topic based on your own personal values. When you choose to write a book on a topic that satisfies those values, you can be sure it will be a great topic and worth writing about – for you!

Let's start. Ask yourself the following three questions and write the answers on a piece of paper, or into your Sure-fire Book Proposal Workbook. Write each answer as a word or a short statement. Later, when your answers are combined within a single sentence, you'll find a topic that's worth writing a book about.

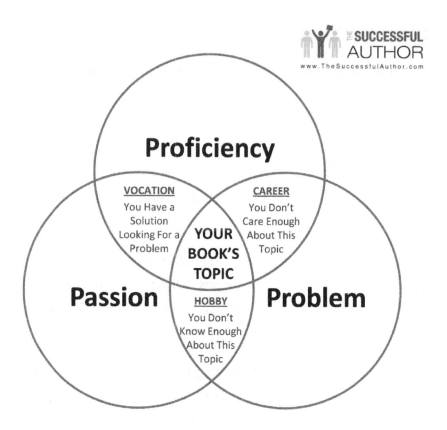

1. Problem

What's the one problem that you feel strongly about and that you want to solve? One that makes you thump the table or shout at the TV.

2. Passion

What are you most passionate about? Something that you love doing and would miss if you had to give it up.

3. Proficiency

What's your particular proficiency? This should be something you're really good at. For example, something that's easy for you to do, but your friends always need your help with. Consider what you are an expert in, or what knowledge, experience, skill, expertise or belief you have that could benefit the lives of other people.

Now take a moment to combine your three answers, by simply selecting one word or phrase from each of the three 'P's and incorporating these words or statements into a single sentence. Write it on a piece of paper or into your Sure-fire Book Proposal Workbook. For example, you could start with the format that I use with my aspiring authors (just fill in the blanks with the answers to the three questions).

I want to use my (passion for) ....

and my (proficiency in) ....

to ....

(the problem of) ....

After completing these three 'P's, you should be much clearer on what's important to you, and that you also feel passionate about, that is something you love and are good at doing.

Optional Activity. You could refine this sentence into a more detailed 'personal statement' about your reason for writing a book, since you will later use this personal statement in the section of your book called 'About the author'. Write this down on a piece of paper for later. Even better would be to fill in your Sure-fire Book Proposal Workbook as you work through each chapter of this book.

Choose Your Book's Topic

Here's how to select a specific book topic that's right for you. Take the sentence or personal statement that you've just created and summarise it in one to three words.

I know it's not easy, but it's worth the effort – it will make your book more successful.

The **SUCCESSFUL** AUTHOR *Strategic Book Topic*

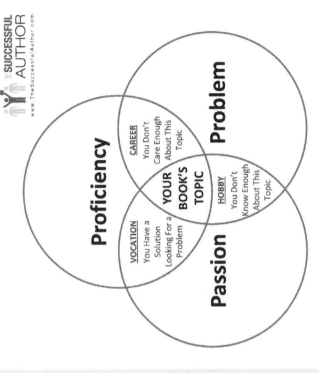

THE **SUCCESSFUL** AUTHOR
www.TheSuccessfulAuthor.com

Proficiency

Problem

Passion

CAREER
You Don't Care Enough About This Topic

VOCATION
You Have a Solution Looking For a Problem

YOUR BOOK'S TOPIC

HOBBY
You Don't Know Enough About This Topic

1. What one **PROBLEM** gets you really fired up? What is it that frustrates you, makes you shout at the TV, or thump the table? Would people pay to solve it?

2. What do you DO that you're most **PASSIONATE** about? What do you love, and would miss if you had to give it up?

3. What do you DO that you are really **PROFICIENT** at? What's easy for you to do well, but friends and colleagues always ask you to help with?

4. Use the sentence template below to combine your three answers. Now summarise it into a 1-3 word topic for your book.
(Note: This is not your book's title!)

"I want to use my (passion for) .... and (proficiency in) ...
.... (the problem of) ....
to .... "

Take this pithy topic and try it out - test it on someone by saying it aloud. How does it sound? Make a note of what they say about it – their view is important.

Yes, I know, it's difficult!

But it's worth the effort, because the result will help create the perfect topic for your book. Your motivation will always remain strong if you base your book's topic on the results of this exercise.

Now try it on someone else and make a note of what they say too. Then do it all over again!

When you have asked **at least** three people for feedback, make your final choice and write it down.

Having chosen your final Book Topic, write it in the WHAT section of the Sure-fire Book Proposal Workbook at the end of this chapter or back of the book.

Optional Activity. If you have time, you could also use Google's Keyword Tool, or an equivalent, to find related/ similar ideas, so that you can refine your chosen topic, based on what people are specifically searching for online. Write these ideas on a piece of paper, or into your Sure-fire Book Proposal Workbook, and don't forget to update your Book Topic in the WHAT section of the workbook.

In some cases, your book topic will make a very good book title. In others, it will need a little 'tweaking' and refinement to align with the topic itself.

For example, you might have a serious topic like 'How to Write a Book', but feel it needs to be livened up a bit: so you might change it to 'Write Your eBook in a Weekend!'

Contrary to popular practice, I truly believe that you should include your choice of book title in your book proposal. Your title is the single most important part of your book. In fact, it's the only part of the book that everyone reads; sadly, that occasionally applies to the people who've actually bought the book! So please don't listen to the book coaches who foolishly suggest ignoring the book's title and tell you that one will mysteriously 'pop into your head' as you write your manuscript. The book and its title are very closely intertwined, so the title should be included in your book proposal right from the start.

The better the picture of your book that you have in your mind as you write it, the closer you will get to achieving your goal. Remember: focus is everything. For example, a key habit (No 2) that Stephen Covey described in his famous book, *The 7 Habits of Highly Successful People*, was 'Begin with the end in mind!'

Now write your Topic-related book title in the WHAT section of your Sure-fire Book Proposal Workbook at the end of this chapter or back of the book..

Summary

In this chapter, we've looked at secret number one: to know WHAT to write about.

This space is for your notes and thoughts.

You should now write some notes and pin them up where you can see them while you're writing your book.

Better still; complete the relevant sections of the Sure-fire Book Proposal Workbook at the end of this chapter or back of the book. As you complete each chapter and learn how to avoid each mistake, you will find that there's a section in the workbook for you to write down your answer. Then they will all be in one place for you to review before doing any writing.

If you'd prefer not to write in the book, you may download a copy of the workbook from:

www.TheSuccessfulAuthor.com/resources

Knowing the secrets of successful authors will help you to avoid the mistakes made by unsuccessful authors. But, clearly, we can't cover everything that you need to know and do within a book. That's why we run group workshops and a series of online webinars. These are designed to walk you through our Sure-fire Book Proposal process. They are designed to drill down into the essential details of your WHAT, WHO, WHY, HOW, WHEN, WHERE, WHICH and can provide you with valuable feedback on how you can improve your proposal - and your book.

Remember, it's much faster and easier to refine a book proposal before you start writing your book than it is to rewrite your whole book after it's finished.

If you'd like to discover more about our webinars, workshops or coaching programmes, please visit:

www.TheSuccessfulAuthor.com

NOTES: Secret 1: WHAT to write about

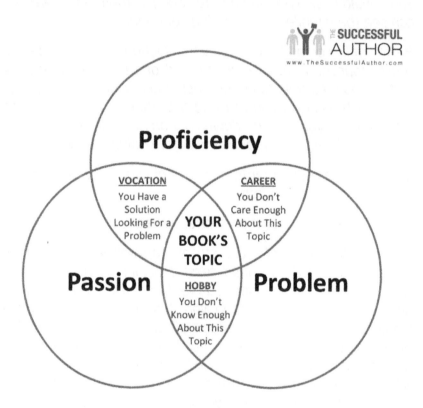

Book topic

What **Problem** do you want to solve?
What's the one problem that you feel strongly about?

What's Your **Passion**?
What do you love that you'd miss if you had to give it up?

What's Your **Proficiency**?
What's easy for you, but friends always ask for help with?

Turn these words or statements into a sentence.

I want to use my passion for

....

and my proficiency in

....

to

....

the problem of

....

So, My TOPIC is

....

My topic-related book title is:

Now use one of the following beginnings to write a paragraph as your author's personal statement.

(maximum of 70 words).

"I believe that...."
"I think..."
"What really annoys me is..."

SECRET 2
WHO TO WRITE FOR

Secret number two is to know WHO to write for. Unsuccessful authors often make the mistake of writing for the wrong reader or even for no reader!

This means that their message never reaches their intended audiences and they never get the results they'd expected. To avoid this, authors need to have a crystal-clear idea of their book's target readership. Unsuccessful authors are often too introverted and end up writing their books for themselves and forgetting to consider other readers. People exactly like the author may find such a book interesting. Unfortunately, that means that the book may have a readership of just one!

Successful authors are good at marketing. They are very specific and define all the characteristics of their potential readerships in great detail, so that they can work out why potential readers would want to read a book on the author's topic. Then they design their book's title and chapters to satisfy those readers' exact requirements. The goal is for a book's target readership to be overjoyed because they have found a book that was exactly what they were looking for. But to achieve this, you must be focused on a specific type of reader.

To avoid making the mistake of writing for the wrong reader or for no reader at all, you'll need to use two techniques. I call the first one 'Types of Reader' and the second 'My Perfect Reader'. When you have finished, you will know your ideal reader very well. You will know what book topics they would buy and for how much, why they would buy it and, more specifically, what would motivate them to buy the particular book that you're writing.

'For me, the most important part of this book was when I worked out who my reader was in detail. I'd had a rough idea and a lot of passion that I wanted to get my message 'out there' but no more than that. The process of getting inside my perfect reader's head was really useful and it made such a difference to my ability to focus as I wrote my book. If I later got lost and started to waffle, then I just went back to my perfect reader's profile and refocused myself to write for that person. Very helpful. And now, it's amazing that that 'perfect reader' that I wrote my book for is exactly the person who now buys my published book. And they even write brilliant book reviews for me on Amazon, because my book 'hit the spot' for them.'

Helen Turier, RGN MAR
Resilience and Wellbeing Practitioner, trainer and author of four books: Bounce-back Ability, Get Back on Your Feet Again, Managing Pressure and Change Effectively, and Discover How Your Lifestyle Could be Killing You
www.helenturier.com

More importantly, if you design your book correctly, you can even predict what they will need to do after they've read your book. That can be a great follow-on business opportunity for an author who wants to increase the quantity of products sold or the number of coaching clients.

Type of Reader

First of all, you need to determine the type of reader that would find your book topic interesting enough to buy it. Here are some great things for you to consider. Use them to define the general type of reader that you want your book to attract.

Demographic profile

Marketers typically combine several variables to define a demographic profile of a group of people in which they're interested. A demographic profile, sometimes referred to as 'a demographic', provides enough information about the typical members of a group to create a mental picture of them (see Wikipedia for more details). For example, an author might want to write a book for a specific type of reader, such as one who is single, female, middle-class, aged 18 to 24, with a university education. Note that these are characteristics that can be verified. Once this reader profile is constructed, authors can use it to develop a marketing strategy.

Common factors used to define demographics are age, gender, income level, race and ethnicity, home ownership, employment status, and even location (see Wikipedia for more details). However, authors should feel free to add other variables to this list, if it gives them a better mental picture of their chosen target readership.

Consider the following list of attributes about your ideal readership (please add to it, if you wish) and write the relevant answers on a piece of paper or in your Sure-fire Book Proposal Workbook.

- **Age**
- **Gender**
- **Annual income**
- **Nationality/ethnicity**
- **Standard of education**
- **Geographic location**
- **Working/unemployed**
- **Value of mortgage debt**
- **Monthly outgoings**
- **Own home/rented**
- **Lives alone/shares with family/shares with friends**
- **Married/separated/divorced/single**
- **Other factors.**

Psychographic profile

Marketers also combine several other variables to define a psychographic profile of a group of people in which they're interested. Psychographics is the study of personality, values, beliefs, attitudes, interests, lifestyle activities, opinions, behaviours, etc. This tells us WHY people do things.

These variables can be difficult to measure or verify directly, because they can sometimes be inferred only from a person's resulting behaviour.

Consider the following list of attributes about your ideal readership (you can add to it, if you wish) and write the answers that are relevant to you on a piece of paper or in your Sure-fire Book Proposal Workbook.

- **Personality**
- **Values**
- **Beliefs**
- **Attitudes**
- **Interests**
- **Lifestyle activity**
- **Opinions**
- **Behaviours**
- **Dreams and goals**
- **Other factors.**

Ideal Reader

Demographic and psychographic profiles are often combined and used together. For example, the people referred to as the 'baby boom generation' are defined by both their demographic variables (classifying individuals based on age) and their psychographic variables, such as their attitudes and behaviours [according to Wikipedia].

Now that you have selected a broad category of readership, you can focus much more specifically on defining your Perfect Reader. The best way to do this is to select a real person, who meets most of the criteria you selected from the two types of profile you've created, to represent your book's perfect readership. You select a specific person who fits your reader profile in order to represent the ideal person you would want to buy or read your book.

You'll need to make a note of the following factors:

- **Name**
- **Situation**
- **Specific problems and challenges**
- **Likely objections to solving these problems**
- **Real quotes, for example what they've said about their life**
- **Attitude to your book's topic.**

Obviously, it's a good idea to select someone who is not only the type of reader you want, but preferably someone you already know very well. That means you can 'get into their head', or 'step into their shoes', as you begin to design your book specifically for them.

So let's go through all these factors one by one. Try to use each of them to define your ideal reader more precisely.

Reader's name

- Select a specific person to represent the ideal reader of your book (or make up a composite person from those you know) and write their name on a piece of paper or in your Sure-fire Book Proposal Workbook.

- Add a photo of them to your computer screen or to a 'vision board'. It's important to place it so that you can see it while you're writing your book – for them.

Reader's situation

Imagine you could put yourself in your perfect reader's situation:

- **How do they feel about their life, and the world in general?**
- **What goes on in their life; what are they 'up to'?**
- **What's their day like?**

Write your answers on a piece of paper or in your Sure-fire Book Proposal Workbook. You'll need them later.

Reader's problems and challenges

Imagine you could put yourself into your perfect reader's situation:

- **What's bothering them, in the context of your book's topic?**
- **What gives them sleepless nights - and why?**
- **List their three main problems.**
- **Which of these is their biggest problem?**

Write your answers on a piece of paper or in your Sure-fire Book Proposal Workbook. You'll need them later.

Reader's objections to your solutions

Consider the most common objections your reader would raise if they were to be offered your solution to their big problem, such as:

- **Insufficient time**
- **Lack of money**
- **I don't believe it will work**
- **I don't believe it will work for me**
- **I don't trust you**
- **I don't need it.**

Make a list of your answers to each of those objections. Write your answers on a piece of paper or in your Sure-fire Book Proposal Workbook. You'll need them later.

Reader's attitude to your book topic

What is your reader's attitude to the topic of your book? For example, is it positive or negative? How does your reader feel about their level of expertise regarding your book's topic? For example, would they see themselves as beginners or at the same level of expertise as you, the author? Write your answers on a piece of paper or in your Sure-fire Book Proposal Workbook. You'll need them later.

Reader's quotations

Get some real quotations from your chosen ideal reader, for example from memory if you've known them for a while, or just ask them how they feel about your topic.

You could extract quotations from interviews or perhaps clip them from newspapers, magazines or blogs, and so on.

It's best if they're from your specified reader, but you could use quotations from someone similar, if necessary.

Write your answers on a piece of paper or in your Sure-fire Book Proposal Workbook. You'll need them later.

Reader's story

Imagine you could just step into your perfect reader's shoes and feel as they do about their situation and your book's topic. Write a short, half-page story about how the 'little voices' in their head describe their life and how you might feel about it. Perhaps you could use the voice recorder on your mobile phone and then transcribe it later. Just let it flow, it doesn't have to make perfect sense to be good enough.

Write it down on a piece of paper or in your Sure-fire Book Proposal Workbook.

Well done! I hope you have a much clearer idea of WHO to write for. You now know your potential readership and you should feel better able to write specifically for them. Remember, unsuccessful authors don't do any of this!

We'll use all this information later.

> Now write a one- or two-sentence summary that defines your Perfect Reader, and then write it in the WHO section of your Sure-fire Book Proposal Workbook at the end of this chapter or back of the book.

Summary

In this chapter, we've looked at secret number two - to know WHO to write for.

You should now write some notes and pin them up where you can see them while you're writing your book.

Better still; complete the relevant sections of the Sure-fire Book Proposal Workbook at the end of this chapter or back of the book. As you complete each chapter and learn how to avoid each mistake, you will find that there's a section in the workbook for you to write down your answer. Then they will all be in one place for you to review before doing any writing.

If you'd prefer not to write in the book, you may download a copy of the workbook from:

www.TheSuccessfulAuthor.com/resources

Knowing the secrets of successful authors will help you to avoid the mistakes made by unsuccessful authors. But, clearly, we can't cover everything that you need to know and do within a book. That's why we run group workshops and a series of online webinars. These are designed to walk you through our Sure-fire Book Proposal process. They are designed to drill down into the essential details of your WHAT, WHO, WHY, HOW, WHEN, WHERE, WHICH and provide you with valuable feedback on how you can improve your proposal - and your book.

Remember, it's much faster and easier to refine a book proposal before you start writing your book than it is to rewrite your whole book after it's finished.

If you'd like to discover more about our webinars, workshops or coaching programmes, please visit:

www.TheSuccessfulAuthor.com

NOTES: Secret 2: WHO to write for
Type of reader

Reader's demographic profile.

```


```

Reader's psychographic profile.

```


```

Your 'ideal reader'

Reader's name(s) (Attach their photograph later).

```


```

Reader's situation (Life, how do they feel about it?).

```


```

Reader's problems and challenges.

1.

2.

3.

Reader's objections to solving these problems.

☐ Insufficient time.

☐ Lack of money.

☐ I don't believe it will work.

☐ I don't believe it will work for me.

☐ I don't trust you.

☐ I don't need it.

Make a list of your answers to each of those objections.

Reader's attitude to your book's topic.

Sample of quotations made by your readers.
What they've said about their life.

[ ]

Reader's story.
Get into rapport, then record it.

[ ]

SECRET 3

WHY YOUR READERS BUY BOOKS

 **S**ecret number three is to know WHY your readers buy books Unsuccessful authors can't promise that their book will deliver what their reader wants or needs, because they don't know what that is - so why would the reader buy it?

Aspiring authors may know their book's topic, and they may even know about their perfect reader. But if they don't know exactly what motivates their reader (they don't know what their reader's problem is), then their book will have a theme about which the reader won't necessarily care.

The reader's psychographic profile will help the author to determine WHY the reader may be motivated to buy their book. Unsuccessful authors give the reader's personality very little thought and are seldom crystal clear about what their reader wants (not necessarily the same as what they need). So authors end up giving their readers too much information, too little information or even the wrong information. I believe that people only ever buy solutions to problems, not books. Think about it...

To avoid making this mistake, aspiring authors should focus specifically on satisfying the needs of their perfect reader. Then, if they can design their book to solve their reader's biggest problem, their reader will definitely be interested in reading it!

Personally, whenever designing a project, I always use a technique, which converts customers' problems to promises, called User-needs

Analysis. I evolved this technique from many sources years ago, while a business consultant and systems analyst, then refined it when I studied marketing design as part of my MBA. Now I use it everywhere. I teach it to all my authors, because it's well proven and it really works. Very quickly, you'll discover why your reader will read (or buy) your book.

Converting Problems to Promises

Here's what you'll do; it's very simple. You're going to work out what problem keeps your reader awake at night. Then you'll devise a solution to that problem which is based on your experience, topic knowledge and insight into your reader's profile. Then you'll write a book about that solution. I said it was simple!

The first step is to ask your perfect reader what their biggest problems are. If you're not in a position to ask directly, then imagine you are yourself the perfect reader of the topic you've chosen for your book (do this even if you have already asked them directly). Now decide what your reader's biggest problem is. Frame this problem as if it were a question, for example starting with:

What / Who / Why / How / When / Where do I ...?

Then you simply need to answer this question and turn the answer into a promise. That promise becomes the underlying theme that should recur throughout your book.

For example, assume your topic is 'how to write books'. Your perfect reader might be a small business-owner, whose problem is that they're struggling during the recession. They might ask the question 'How do I compete for work during an economic downturn?' In this case, your answer might be 'People pay more to hire an expert because they're more effective. All experts write books, so anyone who writes a book is an expert.' Therefore, your promise could then be, 'If you write a book, you'll get more work because you'll be perceived as the expert in your field.' And that becomes the theme of your book. All the information, points, statistics, examples, testimonials, and so on, contained in your book should focus on that theme.

Alternatively, your perfect readers might be knowledgeable specialists or corporate employees who want to raise their profiles before leaving to become self-employed consultants. They might have the problem that they don't believe they have time to write a book. So their question might be, 'Where do I find time to write a book?' In this case, your answer could be, 'Anyone can write a book fast, if they follow a proven system.' And perhaps your promise would be, 'Anyone can write a book in 90 days.' That promise then becomes the main theme of your book and you would write about timescales, diligent effort and effective planning.

Here are the three steps in the process of converting problems to promises:

- **Identify your reader's biggest problem**
- **Solve your reader's problem**
- **Formulate your book's promise.**

Identify your reader's big problem

'A problem well stated is a problem half-solved.'

Christopher Howard,
lifestyle and wealth strategist

This first step is to ask your perfect reader what their biggest problems are and write them down. If you're not in a position to ask them, then you must guess. You can do this by imagining that you are the perfect reader of the topic you've chosen for your book (do this even if you have already asked them directly).

It should be easy, because you've already worked out your perfect reader's demographics and psychographics. You've even created a perfect reader's profile and selected someone you know personally to represent your perfect reader and written all this into your Sure-fire Book Proposal Workbook. Got it? Good.

While imagining that you are your perfect reader, close your eyes and recall what you know about their situation. What are their problems and challenges? Try to think about how they typically spend their day. Imagine hearing the little voices in their head, the ones that continually tell them how their life is going.

What problems do they have? Write them all down. Then, think about these problems. Which of these is the big one, the one that keeps your readers awake at night? Now write down that one big problem which gives them sleepless nights, the one that they'd pay to solve!

But remember your book proposal is not about you, it's about them, so write it in their words. This insight is your single most important resource as an author.

Write your reader's Big Problem in the WHY section of your Sure-fire Book Proposal Workbook at the end of this chapter or back of the book.

Now you need to convert your reader's biggest problem into a single question, so that you can help them to solve it. Ask yourself, 'What do they need to know and how would they ask me?'

Imagine if you were your own perfect reader. What would you want to know, to get what you need to solve this big problem? Write it down in the form of a question. But remember it's not about you; it's about them, so write it in their words.

For example, a great question would probably start with, "How do I ...?" rather than with, "What should I...?"

Write your Reader's Question on a piece of paper or into your Sure-fire Book Proposal Workbook.

> **Optional Activity.** If you want to move up to the next level, then you could use Google's Keyword Tool (or an equivalent)

to refine the phrasing of this question, based on how many people are searching online for answers.

Solve your reader's problem

What do you already know about your reader's problem, based on your experience, knowledge of your topic, and insight into their profile? Use this knowledge to come up with your answer to their question. That answer becomes your solution to their biggest problem.

Now, imagine having told them about your solution to their problem, but they ask for clarification, for example 'What do you mean?' Your response might be:

- **'I believe that ....'**
- **'The truth is ...'**
- **Focusing statements that make their question clearer**
- **Reassurances that they need**
- **Generic or universal points about their question**
- **Your point of view regarding common mis-apprehensions about your topic**
- **Your views of 'experts' in the field.**

Your responses are the very things that your book will also have to address, in order for your reader to properly understand your solution. They will also be useful as chapter headings; or even headlines or bullet points when you write marketing literature for your book, for example the cover blurb, the book description on Amazon, article headlines for book extracts. Write down your notes on Solutions and Responses in your Sure-fire Book Proposal Workbook.

Formulate your book's promise

Now turn your answer into a promise. What you're trying to do is make a promise of a favourable outcome, which your reader could achieve by reading your book. Your book must promise to solve their main problem, the one that keeps them awake at night. Your promise should not take the form of a question. For example, it should start with something like:

'Don't …', 'I can …', 'You can …', 'You will …', 'I guarantee that …'

Write your book's promise in the WHY section of your Sure-fire Book Proposal at the end of this chapter or back of the book.

The promise should clearly appear somewhere on your book's cover. Either as the title or subtitle, or prominently on the back cover.

Optional Activity. If you want to move up to the next level, then you could refine your promise by looking on Amazon's book pages to see what other books in your topic area are promising.

This promise becomes the main theme of your book and should recur frequently.

Write your book's main theme in the WHY section of your Sure-fire Book Proposal at the end of this chapter or back of the book.

Why Your Reader Will Buy

Your book's promise is the reason why your readers will read or buy your book. Simple!

Knowing your perfect reader's personality and motivators, as you do (from their psychographic profile), you're definitely going to print your promise on the cover of your book – because it will help them decide whether to buy or not.

'The British Airports Authority and the travel website Expedia, jointly commissioned the poll of 2,100 people... One in three has bought a book just to look intelligent... Some consumers hedge their bets by keeping two titles on the go - one an impressive book to show other people, the other an escapist work to enjoy.'

John Ezard,
The Guardian, Monday 24 October 2005

You could now carry out some research by ooking on Amazon to see how popular your book's topic is and at what price similar titles are pitched. Having researched the value readers place on your solution, you should now be able estimate the price your perfect reader would pay to resolve their big problem.

Write your estimated selling price in the WHY section of your Sure-fire Book Proposal at the end of this chapter or back of the book.

Summary

In this chapter, we've looked at secret number three - to know WHY your readers buy books.

This space is for your notes and thoughts.

You should now write some notes and pin them up where you can see them while you're writing your book.

Better still; complete the relevant sections of the Sure-fire Book Proposal Workbook at the end of this chapter or back of the book. As you complete each chapter and learn how to avoid each mistake, you will find that there's a section in the workbook for you to write down your answer. Then they will all be in one place for you to review before doing any writing.

If you'd prefer not to write in the book, you may download a copy of the workbook from:

www.TheSuccessfulAuthor.com/resources

Knowing the secrets of successful authors will help you to avoid the mistakes made by unsuccessful authors. But, clearly, we can't cover everything that you need to know and do within a book. That's why we run group workshops and a series of online webinars. These are designed to walk you through our Sure-fire Book Proposal process. They are designed to drill down into the essential details of your WHAT, WHO, WHY, HOW, WHEN, WHERE, WHICH and provide you with valuable feedback on how you can improve your proposal - and your book.

Remember, it's much faster and easier to refine a book proposal before you start writing your book than it is to rewrite your whole book after it's finished.

If you'd like to discover more about our webinars, workshops or coaching programmes, please visit:

www.TheSuccessfulAuthor.com

NOTES: Secret 3: WHY your readers buy books

Reader's one big problem.

That keeps them awake at night.

What's the key question they would ask you if they could?

What do they need to know?

Your promise

Your answer to your reader's key question.
This is your key message.

Write down six or seven supporting messages.

1.

2.

3.

4.

5.

6.

7

What is your book's promise?

Book's main theme (based on your promise).

Feasible selling price of your book (Check on Amazon).

SECRET 4

HOW TO DESIGN YOUR BOOK

Secret number four is to know HOW to design your book. Most aspiring authors don't know how to write a book. They usually try to start writing at page one, then continue until they decide they're finished.

This makes it difficult to promote the book in advance of publication, since its final contents and completion date won't be known until it's finished. In addition, this approach means that the book's structure and contents must be designed on the fly and previous work may need to be revised, or discarded, as the topic evolves or the author changes their mind about 'what's in' and 'what's not'.

This make-it-up-as-you-go approach is seldom effective. These books take a long time to write and, in many cases, may never be completed. Successful authors know how to design and write a book correctly and it takes them a fraction of the time to write than it would otherwise.

'Do your research and homework before you start to write. The key to writing a book is to start. Writing is one thing that you cannot get worse at by doing it.'

Brian Tracy,
bestselling author

'I think people experience a surge of overwhelm when they consider everything that's involved in writing a book. So I would say the biggest thing I took away from your one-day Book Design workshop was simply the fact that one could design a whole book in a day! Yes, that is definitely the biggest thing that you take away. I remember thinking – WHAT? Are you crazy? One day to design my book – and then I will be completely ready to write it? But I was ... and I did! It was nothing short of remarkable. Thank you, Kevin!'

Jennie Harland-Khan
Mentor, speaker, and author of I'm BACK! How to get your passion, purpose and identity back when your kids go to school
www.jenniehk.com

Successful authors obviously know how to write a book. They are clear about their book's purpose and topic and they identify its goals and its component parts. By defining what their book will achieve, for whom, and the method by which it will be written at the very start means they can change the design and get it right beforehand. Therefore, they won't need to rewrite their manuscript to get it right afterwards. That is, they create a rigid Bullet-proof Book Design Specification. They use this as a prototype that they can test to ensure their book will achieve its goals. Then they write their manuscript from the design, making sure it turns out exactly as they designed it. You see, it's a fact of life that if you don't know where you're going, then any road will get you there. And you might not like where you end up!

A major part of successfully writing a book is to work diligently from a good book design. Designing your book is achieved by following a systematic, step-by-step process.

Bullet-proof Book Design Specification

Here are seven components of a book design specification. I help my authors make choices about each, so they can specify their book's design in their book proposal.

1. **Category of book.** All published books need to be categorised to help a potential reader narrow their search.

2. **Type of book.** Examples of book types could be: new information, reference material, self-help, how-to, compilations.

3. **Book's internal structure.** To get this right you could, for example, consider using techniques such as Kipling's Six Serving Men, 4MAT, the 'Rule of Three', AIDA Sales Process, Extended Sales Process, or Collaboration. [7]

---

7   These techniques are covered in more detail during the author's webinars and workshops.

4. **Book title.** Spend time with your perfect reader or someone who knows your topic - preferably both - and brainstorm some book titles, based on your book's promise.

5. **Cover design elements.** Everyone judges a book by its cover. So spend time with your perfect reader or someone who knows your topic - preferably both - to brainstorm some cover ideas. Don't forget to include your book's promise.

6. **Table of contents.** Choose your chapter titles, based on what your readers need to know or what you want to say about your topic. For example, you could use your seven answers to your reader's biggest question. The lower-level sections and subsections will be defined later, after your book proposal is completed, during the design of your book's prototype.

7. **Quality criteria.** You need to decide the rules you will use to check that your manuscript is complete, consistent, and meets your reader's expectations for the type of book you're writing.

Plan to Write a Book

A book's design defines the book: it's your goal for what the book will be like. But, without a writing plan, your design is simply a piece of paper. A book's design and writing plan are interrelated; you can't make a plan without first creating the design.

'A goal without a plan is just a wish!'

Antoine de Saint-Exupéry,
French writer (1900-1944)

I always recommend that authors follow four steps.

1. They specify their book (for example, in their Sure-fire Book Proposal workbook).

2. They decide what it will include and (equally importantly) what it won't (for example, in their bullet-proof book design).

3. They create a writing schedule (for example, the timetable within their foolproof writing plan)

4. Finally, they follow their writing plan and write about what they've designed until they're finished. They come to me, because I hold them accountable to it.

It's essential for authors to resist the urge to change their book's design as they write it.

Book Design Specification

'I thought your Book Design Workshop was great! The fact that, in just one day, we broke down the whole book to the level of detail needed to start writing the very next day was just awesome.'

Alun Richards
Author of two books, The Seven Critical Website Mistakes and Fire Your Webmaster
www.yourwebmasterisfired.co.uk

So let's start specifying your book's design. Actually creating your book's design from this specification will come later, so for now we'll just deal with specifying it within the book proposal.

Category of book

All published books need to be categorised, based on their topic, to help a prospective reader to narrow their search, both online and in the bookshop. It also helps bookshops to place related books together on the shelves.

Here is a list of typical non-fiction book categories from which you could choose. Some publishers have their own categories. Further examples can be found online. Some of these types could be applied to business books, some not. Normally, you would select only one category for a book.

- **Arts & Photography**
- **Biographies & Memoirs**
- **Business & Economics**
- **Computers & Internet**
- **Cooking**
- **Crafts & Hobbies**
- **Diet & Health**
- **Education & Language**
- **Engineering**
- **Entertainment**
- **History**
- **Home & Garden**
- **Law**
- **Medicine & Science**
- **Parenting & Families**
- **Pets**
- **Reference**
- **Self-improvement**
- **Sports & Adventure**
- **Travel.**

Select a book category that best suits your topic. Write it in the HOW section of your Sure-fire Book Proposal workbook at the end of this chapter or back of the book.

Type of book

Here is a list of five types of book that you could select; there are others. The type of book is a useful way of describing it when speaking to others (and to yourself!).

Examples can be found on any bookshelf. Any of these types could be applied to either business books or non-business books.

- **New Information.** Author is either a researcher or an expert on the book's topic. Normally it is read from start to finish.

- **Reference manual.** Author is a researcher or expert on the book's topic. The reader can dip in to the text wherever they like.

- **Self-help.** Author needs to be an 'expert' on the book's topic. May be divided into stand-alone sections, or take the reader step-by-step through a process that starts at the first chapter and finishes at the last chapter.

- **How-to.** Author needs to be an 'expert' on the book's topic and gives the reader instructions. The reader needs to have a clear outcome, or promise. Normally the book takes the reader step-by-step through a process, starting at the first chapter and finishing at the last chapter.

- **Compilation**, that is, there is more than one author. It's essential to have a connecting theme: the author is an interviewer, key person, researcher, or editor of others' contributions.

> Choose the Type of book that best suits your topic, your ideal reader, and your personal preference. Write it in the HOW section of your Sure-fire Book Proposal Workbook at the end of this chapter or back of the book.

Book's internal structure

Here is a list of seven, well-proven internal structures that I recommend[8] for any non-fiction book:

- **Kipling's Six Serving Men**
- **4MAT**
- **The 'Rule of Three'**
- **Simple Sales Process**
- **AIDA Sales Process**
- **Extended Sales Process**
- **Collaboration**

Many other examples can be found on any bookshelf. Any of these structures could be applied to either business books or non-business books.

Here are the two I used for this book's internal structure.

---

8   These techniques are covered in more detail during the author's webinars and workshops.

Kipling's Six Serving Men

As you will have noticed, this book uses Rudyard Kipling's questions as the basis for its internal structural design. That is, each chapter is based on one of Kipling's six questions:

- **Who?**
- **What?**
- **Where?**
- **When?**
- **Why?**
- **How?**

These simple questions can be applied in any sequence that suits your topic. The questions lend themselves to forming a book's overall structure, or you could even use all of them within each chapter.

'Writing this book has been an amazing experience. Not least, because I was a member of Kevin's fabulous Successful Author Academy. Full of brilliant people; each of whom succeeded in writing their own book within the same 90 days. Thank goodness for our Facebook group; those encouraging posts really kept me on track when I needed it most.

Helen Turier, RGN MAR
Resilience and Wellbeing Practitioner, trainer and author of four books: Bounce-back Ability, Get Back on Your Feet Again, Managing Pressure and Change Effectively, and Discover How Your Lifestyle Could be Killing You
www.helenturier.com

4MAT System

To accommodate people's different learning styles, I suggest authors use the 4MAT system (developed by Bernice McCarthy[9]).

1. **Meaning** - Why?

2. **Concepts** - What?

3. **Skills** - How?

4. **Adaptations** - What if? (What else, or What next?)

I avoid the theoretical complexities and use a very simplified version, whereby the answers to four questions are presented to a reader or listener in the sequence shown below. You can apply this method either to your whole book (one question per chapter) or to a single chapter (all four categories appearing in the same chapter).

For example, within this book, I first state the title and define each secret. Then I follow the 4MAT system to present my point:

1. **Why** something happens and why it's a problem.

2. **What** the secret is to avoiding it (touching on the key points of the solution).

3. **How** to avoid it (for instance, give some practical points, steps or examples).

4. **What Next** (for example, I ask my readers to add their answers to their Book Proposal Workbook and explain that,

---

9   More details: http://www.aboutlearning.com/what-is-4mat

if they need more help with a detailed solution, they should book onto one of my webinars or workshops).

> Now select the Book's internal structure that best suits your book's topic, your perfect reader and your own personal preference. Write it in the HOW section of your Sure-fire Book Proposal Workbook at the end of this chapter or back of the book.

Book title

Spend time with someone who knows your topic or ideal reader (preferably both), in order to brainstorm some great book titles. Here are some pointers that I usually recommend to my own authors:

- **Your book's title should make readers say 'I want that!'**
- **Your subtitle should tell readers what your book is about.**

A cynic once told me there are only five book concepts to consider. I'll leave it to you to decide for yourself.

1. Encourage the reader's dreams.

2. Justify their failures.

3. Calm their fears.

4. Confirm their suspicions.

5. Undermine their enemies.

Choose a final book title that best suits your topic, your ideal reader and personal preference. And write them in the HOW section of your Sure-fire Book Proposal Workbook at the end of this chapter or back of the book.

Cover design elements

Yes, it's true! Everyone judges a book by its cover. Here's something to think about:

'On average, a book-store browser spends eight seconds looking at the front cover and fifteen seconds looking at the back cover.'

The Wall Street Journal[10]

Spend time with your ideal reader or someone who knows your topic (preferably both) to brainstorm some cover ideas. Here are some pointers that I recommend to my own authors:

---

10   Source: http://www.parapublishing.com/sites/para/resources/statistics.cfm

- An eye-catching graphic on the front cover will grab the reader's attention.

- A topic-related graphic on the front cover, perhaps a metaphor or stereotype of the topic, will help the reader choose the book.

- Include your ideal reader's biggest problem or question on the back cover to show readers that the book is written for them.

- Include any reader's testimonials or endorsements you have, to help to reassure readers that the book is worth reading (social proof).

- Prominently place your book's promise (to solve the reader's biggest problem) on the back cover, to help close the sale.

Make a note of the Cover design elements that best suit your topic, your ideal reader and your personal preference. Write them in the HOW section of your Sure-fire Book Proposal Workbook at the end of this chapter or back of the book..

Table of contents

Choose three, five or seven chapters in total. Any more than that and your book will become too big and unwieldy to write it quickly.

If it takes more than six or seven weeks (or sometimes even six or seven days for a small book), you may run out of motivation.

- Don't forget to stick to the interior structure you have selected. For example, you might have adopted my Rule of Three to create a minimal structure, comprising an introduction, some chapters and a conclusion.

- Ensure that your chapters all support your promise. For example, you could write a chapter around each of your top answers to your reader's big question.

- Choose each chapter title and its place in the sequence, so that if all the chapter titles were to be strung together into a long sentence it would make sense.

- Choose your chapter topics so they 'stand alone' and can each be read in isolation, or could even be deleted without ruining the whole book.

Write your chapter titles in the HOW section of your Sure-fire Book Proposal Workbook at the end of this chapter or back of the book.

At this stage, don't worry about your chapter's lower-level headings, subheadings and so forth. These are the low-level components of your book's final design; for now we're just specifying the big picture, of what will be in the top level of the contents list.

Summary

In this chapter, we've looked at secret number four - to know HOW to design your book.

This space is for your notes and thoughts.

You should now write some notes and pin them up where you can see them while you're writing your book.

Better still; complete the relevant sections of the Sure-fire Book Proposal Workbook at the end of this chapter or back of the book. As you complete each chapter and learn how to avoid each mistake, you will find that there's a section in the workbook for you to write down your answer. Then they will all be in one place for you to review before doing any writing.

If you'd prefer not to write in the book, you may download a copy of the workbook from:

www.TheSuccessfulAuthor.com/resources

Knowing the secrets of successful authors will help you to avoid the mistakes made by unsuccessful authors. But, clearly, we can't cover everything that you need to know and do within a book. That's why we run group workshops and a series of online webinars. These are designed to walk you through our Sure-fire Book Proposal process. They are designed to drill down into the essential details of your WHAT, WHO, WHY, HOW, WHEN, WHERE, WHICH and provide you with valuable feedback on how you can improve your proposal - and your book.

Remember, it's much faster and easier to refine a book proposal before you start writing your book than it is to rewrite your whole book after it's finished.

If you'd like to discover more about our webinars, workshops or coaching programmes, please visit:

www.TheSuccessfulAuthor.com

NOTES: Secret 4: HOW to design your book

Your book structure

Category of book.

Type of book.

Internal structure type.

Final book title.
To attract attention. (Less than 8 words).

Subtitle.

Explains what it's about. (Less than 16 words).

Cover design elements.

Contents list:

[Title page]

[Copyright page]

Author's other books (optional).

Dedication/Acknowledgements (optional).

Introduction (optional).

Chapter titles

1.

2.

3.

4.

5.

6.

7.

Conclusion

Next steps (Your sales pitch)

About the author and author's personal statement

Book cover

Book title.
To attract attention. (Less than 8 words)

Subtitle.
Explains what it's about. (Less than 16 words)

Rear heading.
Why should I buy this book? Could be Reader's key Question, or your Promise. (Less than 16 words).

Rear blurb.

Why should I buy this book now? Your Key Messages; the Benefits of reading it; could include a testimonial. (Less than 150 words total).

Author's biography and photo.
Why should I listen to you? (Less than 50 words total)

SECRET 5

WHEN TO FINISH WRITING

Secret number five is to know WHEN to finish writing. Some people don't plan ahead; they just make everything up as they go along: does that sound familiar?

Well, too many unsuccessful authors do exactly the same. That means that they don't know how much work will be involved in writing their manuscript. It also means they have no idea when they'll be finished. If the time taken to write their manuscript is not known in advance, then an author can't make any arrangements for managing their time commitments or for scheduling the subsequent publishing, launching or promoting of their book. So, after their manuscript is written, there will be a further delay, because the follow-on services will not have been arranged and will take many months to set up.

Successful authors discover that writing their manuscript is best carried out by following a systematic, step-by-step process. That is, one which enforces a discipline and gives a high degree of predictability to all aspects of the book's production and publishing. The ideal way to know when you will finish writing is to follow a proven plan that has been specifically designed to help authors do all that is required, at the right time, and in the correct sequence.

'A project is not an ongoing activity. It is a one-off process with a clearly defined start and end date, designed to implement a specific scope of work (a design) to achieve a desired outcome. All projects contain a sequence of predetermined tasks intended to create one or more tangible results that will achieve the specific goal of the project.'

Kevin Bermingham

However, your book's design and planning are interrelated; you can't have one without the other. So, assuming you have already created a bullet-proof design for your book, we will deal only with specifying the plan to write the manuscript.

Here's my Strategic Book Framework in nine steps. Only the first six steps are needed to publish the book, the remaining three steps are only needed to exploit the book to create profitable collateral products derived from the book.

Just so you know – this book on the seven secrets of successful authors only covers step one!

1. **Propose.** Specify your intended book's Sure-Fire Strategy in the form of a Book Proposal. By doing this at the start, you can be sure you're going to achieve your strategic goals for the book. That's how we can ensure that it's *THE RIGHT BOOK!*

2. **Prototype.** Create a Bullet-Proof Design containing the name and relationships between of all your book's components - chapters, headings, sub-headings, and so on.

3. **Plan.** Create a Fool-Proof Project Plan of how you will implement your book's design. This includes your daily writing schedule.

4. **Produce.** Follow your Fool-Proof Project Plan's writing schedule to write and review your Persuasive Manuscript so that it exactly matches your Bullet-Proof Design. Be sure to find someone who can motivate you to follow your plan!

5. **Prepare.** Production of your book's print-ready files can only happen after the manuscript is both written and error-free. When it is, this step includes the editing, page design and typesetting that is carried out by technical specialists. The author is then given a proof copy for last minute proofreading in case any typographic errors have crept in.

6. **Publish.** The process of publishing happens after the book's print-ready files have been created and the proof copy approved. The book is assigned one of the publisher's ISBNs so that its source can be tracked. It is then made available for printing and the books in print databases are updated. Six copies are printed and registered with the six legal deposit libraries.

7. **Productise.** Your book contains valuable intellectual property. Much, or all, of it can be extracted and cleverly

re-purposed for other uses. This step is about turning that intellectual property into strategic products that support your goals of clarity, credibility and collateral.

8. **Package**. Having broken up your book into strategic products, the next step is to package them up into appropriate formats, either physical or digital. Some products may be packaged into more than one format. For example, a physical video DVD, audio CD, audio MP3 downloads and a training manual.

9. **Promote.** The book will be distributed for sale to outlets after the book has been published. A number of promotional activities and campaigns may then be carried out to encourage book sales. Often the book may be given pre-publishing advance promotion to build anticipation within the marketplace. The information products, derived from the book, are also promoted; perhaps in their own right, or as components in a training programme, or home study kit.

The **SUCCESSFUL** AUTHOR *Strategic Book Framework*

A Achieve Strategic **CLARITY**

1. PROPOSE
Sure-Fire Strategy

2. PROTOTYPE
Bullet-Proof Design

3. PLAN
Fool-Proof Project

B Boost Personal **CREDIBILITY**

4. PRODUCE
Persuasive Manuscript

5. PREPARE
Publishable Book

6. PUBLISH
The *RIGHT* Book

C Create Profitable **COLLATERAL**

7. PRODUCTISE
Valuable Content

8. PACKAGE
Attractive Collateral

9. PROMOTE
Profitable Sales

Foolproof Writing Plan

It's essential for authors to resist the urge to change the design of their book while they're writing the manuscript. So we build quality criteria and performance measures into the plan to prevent this from happening.

Here are the minimum set of items that should be contained in a foolproof writing plan.

- Writing Strategy (your writing approach and a specification of your planned deliverables. It is based on your book's design).

- Start and end dates (calculated from adding up all the work needed to produce the manuscript).

- Quality and performance criteria (to help you recognise when you've finished).

'You combined project planning with right-brain visioning and, with your use of a "future timeline", was a very effective approach. It really generated motivation to get started on my book.'

Alun Richards
Author of two books, The Seven Critical Website Mistakes and Fire Your Webmaster
www.yourwebmasterisfired.co.uk

A foolproof writing plan is a tool, designed to convert the process of writing of a book into a predictable project. This means that the book's finish date can be predicted and if not acceptable, then the writing can be re-planned and re-scheduled until the author and publisher is satisfied with the outcome.

My own experience is that no project should be allowed to take longer than 90 days. It is by using a predefined, foolproof plan, such as the one I describe in this book, that I have been able to guarantee that every one of my authors will complete the writing and publishing of their books within just 90 days, or less.

'There are two reasons why [projects] commonly fail. The first is lack of planning to ascertain each of the necessary steps. The second is that the project lasts too long and people lose focus. An ideal project should last no more than 90-100 days until completion. If we have longer projects we should refocus individual sub-goals and steps into maximum three-month time intervals.'

MATTA, N. F. and ASHKENAS, R. N.,
'Why good projects fail anyway', *Harvard Business Review* [11]

You won't be able to include a complete foolproof plan in your book proposal. That's because the full plan will be created from your

11   Harvard Business Review, Sep 2003, Volume: 81 Issue: 9 pp.109-114

book's design and you haven't yet carried out the seven hours of design work that's typically required to design a book. So for your book proposal, all you will be able to do is include your plan's quality and performance criteria.

For example, let's assume you plan to have seven chapters and write a modest 4,000-word chapter each week. That means you should also be able to calculate a completion date for each of your chapters and for the overall manuscript; those are your performance criteria. Here are the basic components I recommend including in your foolproof writing plan.

Planning strategy

Lots of people make plans every day, for example:

Do this ..., do that ..., then do this ...!

Even some professional project experts use this method. However, there's a problem: there's a fatal flaw within it. This type of plan is based on planning and scheduling the ACTIVITIES needed to achieve the goal of the project, such as plan-**ing**, write-**ing**, edit-**ing**, and so on - note they are always do-ing words that end in -**ing**.

You see, when we carry out activities, we work **at** doing them; so first of all, they're started, then they're in progress, then they're ten per cent done, then sixty, then ninety ... and so on. But they can never be completed, because there's always a bit more work that could be done to make them better - so the date for one-hundred-per-cent 'done' keeps moving further away. Therefore, our project ends up with a whole lot of work that is all ninety-per-cent done!

Measuring progress, when planning with activities, is a flawed concept. This is because the desired outcome (the activity becoming one hundred per cent completed) can never be achieved.

What is worse, I found that some activities could be planned, but their results can't be measured; only the time spent working is measurable! And because activity percentages are subjective, they're inconsistent; everyone who tries to measure the completion of the work estimates a different percentage value.

As a successful professional project manager for many years, I took a different approach.

When starting a project, I simply identified the final tangible deliverable that the project was designed to produce (for a book, for example, it might be a finished manuscript).

Then I broke that down into smaller and smaller tangible work-products, or components (such as finished chapters). I continued to do this until I had complete list of the project's work-products, which were all much smaller than the final deliverable. I stopped breaking them down into smaller work-products when each of them would take only days or hours to produce (such as a subsection, or even a page). Note that these must all be tangible, so that the completion of each can be measured.

So now, to measure progress, I didn't need to estimate activity completion percentages: I only needed to count how many of these smaller work-products were completed.

Therefore, each work-product on my list was either zero-per-cent or one-hundred-per-cent finished.

When I wanted to measure the project's progress towards completion, I just needed to count the completed work-products and calculate if I was ten, sixty, ninety, or one hundred per cent through my list.

What was even better, someone else could measure the project's progress (by counting the same tangible things) and get the same result as I did.

'This best technique for planning and managing any project is "Product-based Planning" not "Activity-based Planning" and is the only one I use for managing my authors' book projects.'

Kevin Bermingham

For a book-writing project, the author's main tangible deliverable is obviously the finished manuscript, which was created from the book's design. A writing strategy is the approach you will take to write the pages, or sections, or chapters, and so on, until you have a complete book that contains all the components you specified in the book's design.

Cyclic writing strategy

Some writing coaches allow an author's book design to be created, or to change, while the manuscript is being written. Aspiring authors are then advised (foolishly) to wait until they've finished writing the whole manuscript before they seek other people's feedback on its quality. Of course, by then there is not much time left to continue writing, so it may be too late to make any substantial corrections needed to resolve any problems that are found.

I require my authors to adopt what I call a 'Cyclic Writing Strategy'. I insist that they design their book in advance and get their designs checked for errors before they start writing, while it is still simple to make changes. Then I insist that they seek peer feedback on each chapter as it's written, rather than wait for the whole manuscript to be completed.

Designing the book up front means that each chapter is completed just as soon as it's written, and won't need to change later, because of the author's new ideas or second thoughts, while they write subsequent chapters.

In addition, it can be a fearsome thing for an aspiring author to have someone criticise his or her best work. So it's a great idea to practice accepting feedback on a chapter-by-chapter basis, rather than on the whole manuscript. The author then gets the opportunity to learn from early feedback, so they can improve their subsequent chapters. However, with a tight cyclic writing schedule, your chapter review process will be intense! So, be sure to plan it well in advance to avoid missing your deadlines during the weeks ahead.

When to finish writing?

Once you have a plan, the answer's easy. You will finish writing when all the work-products in your foolproof writing plan have been completed; then you can stop and move on to something else.

There's no need, or point, in continuing to write more, when all the components in your writing plan have been completed.

Make a note of your chosen writing strategy in the WHEN section of your Sure-fire Book Proposal Workbook at the end of this chapter or back of the book.

Start and end dates

Publishing and exploiting a book is a project that can be broken down into nine major steps:

1. Proposing

2. Prototyping

3. Planning

4. Producing

5. Preparing

6. Publishing

7. Productising

8. Packaging

9. Promoting

They each have their own start and end dates and each step is dependent on the completion of the preceding step.

Writing a manuscript comes within the producing step. It has fixed boundaries, which will have been specifically defined as quality criteria in the book proposal. The end date is clearly important, for obvious reasons to do with the scheduling of later steps, such as publishing. However, sometimes the start date of the writing step is equally important for aspiring authors who are prone to perpetual planning, or inaction due to procrastination (a fear of failing).

So how does an author calculate these dates?

For an activity-based plan, the author prepares a schedule of the tasks needed to write the manuscript. They are discrete items of work, each being a measurable indicator of progress towards achieving the project's outcome (a finished manuscript). The sum of the time needed for each **task** gives us the time between the start and end dates.

For my recommended, foolproof writing plan (the product-based plan), the author prepares a schedule of completion dates for every work-product that needs to be produced (such as the chapters). These are discrete items of work, completion of each being a measurable indicator of progress towards achieving the project's outcome (a finished manuscript). As before, the sum of the time needed to produce all these **work-products** gives us the time between the start and end dates.

Calculate each chapter's start and end dates, then write the overall start and end date for your book in the WHEN section of your Sure-fire Book Proposal Workbook at the end of this chapter or back of the book.

Quality and performance criteria

If we have created a plan to write a book in the way I've just described, with product-based planning, then we can carry out some measuring of progress towards our targets. But first, we have to decide on the targets: the quality criteria that the writing project must achieve in order to be considered successful. In all practical situations, the word 'quality' is simply defined as being 'fit for purpose'. For example, both a modestly priced bicycle and an expensive Rolls Royce car are of equal quality because they have different purposes.

Think about that!

Now, let's get back to the manuscript's quality.

Firstly, we have to define what we mean by 'completed', because it is one of the most important quality criteria for the manuscript. For example, do we mean simply that we want the manuscript to be finished by a certain date, or does the word 'completion' mean a lot more than that? In fact, your book's quality criteria will have been derived from its design and could read something like this:

> *The manuscript must be posted to the publisher before the end of June this year; it must have between 30,000 and 50,000 words; it must be written on the topic agreed; it must include all seven chapters and each chapter must contain all the headings and subheadings that were specified in the agreed Book Design.*

It's fine having quality criteria, but we also need to adopt an appropriate approach to ensure that we can achieve them.

Here are some tips to ensure that your writing performance will be sufficient to meet your targets.

- Decide on **how much time** you're going to invest on a regular basis. For example, ninety minutes of writing every day or an average of 10 hours each week.

- Measure your **writing performance,** for example 1,000 words per hour or three pages per day, and adjust your situation to achieve it.

- Create a list of your tangible **work-products** and decide how many are to be 'completed' per day, week or month. One example of a completed work-product could be a whole chapter; written, reviewed and self-edited.

- Measure your **completion performance**. Measure how many work-products are 'completed' per day, week or month.

> Make a note of the quality and performance criteria you will adopt and write them in the WHEN section of your Sure-fire Book Proposal Workbook. at the end of this chapter or back of the book.

Summary

In this chapter, we've looked at secret number five - to know WHEN to finish writing.

This space is for your notes and thoughts.

You should now write some notes and pin them up where you can see them while you're writing your book.

Better still; complete the relevant sections of the Sure-fire Book Proposal Workbook at the end of this chapter or back of the book. As you complete each chapter and learn how to avoid each mistake, you will find that there's a section in the workbook for you to write down your answer. Then they will all be in one place for you to review before doing any writing.

If you'd prefer not to write in the book, you may download a copy of the workbook from:

www.TheSuccessfulAuthor.com/resources

Knowing the secrets of successful authors will help you to avoid the mistakes made by unsuccessful authors. But, clearly, we can't cover everything that you need to know and do within a book. That's why we run group workshops and a series of online webinars. These are designed to walk you through our Sure-fire Book Proposal process. They are designed to drill down into the essential details of your WHAT, WHO, WHY, HOW, WHEN, WHERE, WHICH and provide you with valuable feedback on how you can improve your proposal - and your book.

Remember, it's much faster and easier to refine a book proposal before you start writing your book than it is to rewrite your whole book after it's finished.

If you'd like to discover more about our webinars, workshops or coaching programmes, please visit:

www.TheSuccessfulAuthor.com

NOTES: Secret 5: WHEN to finish writing

Writing strategy.

Overall start and end date.

Chapter start and end dates.

Introduction

1.

2.

3.

4.

5.

6.

7.

Conclusion

Quality criteria.

Performance criteria.

SECRET 6

WHERE TO PROMOTE YOUR BOOK

Secret number six is to know WHERE to promote your book. Being successful as an author is not always about high-volume book sales.

There are 200,000 titles a year published in the UK. That is a lot of competition, so it takes a special type of author to hit the mass-market and make money from book royalties.

What is worse, the traditional publishing model is available only to those with a proven track record. Traditional mainstream publishers no longer take on anyone other than the very best, hot-prospect authors; even if they do sign up an unknown, they haven't the money or time to promote them.

So, if a mainstream publishing deal isn't a viable route for you to exploit your book, then what is? How else can you make money from it? Unsuccessful authors have no idea and, when they fail to get the mainstream publishing deal they'd hoped for, they have no idea *where* else to promote their book.

Non-traditional Book Promotion

If planning to make money from publisher's advances and royalties is not the best strategy, how else could you exploit your book?

Most authors have found that there are far more ways of exploiting their new reputation as an expert than just selling books.

Here are some ways to exploit your book yourself once it is published:

- **Leave a legacy.** Simply use your book to 'give something back' to society or to tell your story about overcoming adversity. Promote and sell the book to organisations that value your insights.

- **Become a published expert.** By publishing a book, you will be perceived as the expert in your field. For example, it's common knowledge that people buy from those they know, like and trust. That's why the social media are such effective marketing channels. You could even use your book as your sales brochure or business card.

- **Become a Successful Author.** More than just becoming a published expert, the key being a 'successful author' is to 'productise' your book. This is probably the most effective way for an expert to exploit their book. Just publishing your book will have helped you to achieve more clarity, credibility and collateral (tangible evidence of competence) for yourself and your business. However, we all know that experts can more-easily win more sales and charge premium prices for their time, products and services, unlike their unpublished competitors. This is because when potential clients, or sales prospects, read your book, they'll not only know you better, but they'll understand their own problems better and are likely to be highly motivated to purchase a solution from you. So the successful author will have already 'productised' their book to create products and services 'related' to the book.

The Successful Author ™

Isn't it odd that people who publish a non-fiction book immediately become 'the expert' on that topic? Their opinion suddenly becomes worthwhile and newly respected by their peers; they can also expect to be approached by the media.

Yet, in reality, they've simply packaged their existing skills, knowledge and expertise for the benefit of others. The truth is that they're just ordinary people like you or I.

> 'Experts write books, therefore authors must be experts.'
>
> **Kevin Bermingham**

The best way to exploit your book as a published expert is to develop a simple business strategy in which you create the products or services to provide the solution that your book advocates.

Here are some products to consider creating from your book:

- **Brochure**
- **Flyer**
- **Networking**
- **Website**
- **Download**
- **Articles**
- **Blog Posts**

- **Videos**
- **Seminars**
- **Workshops**
- **Workbooks**

If you've followed my recommendations, you will already be planning to write a book that does just this. I believe that creating a business, based on your book, will transform your life faster than any meagre royalties from selling the book ever would. Here are just three ways in which it can be done:

Turn your book into a training course

Some of my clients have left full-time work to run a training business that they set up. They sell premium-priced seminars and workshops to their perfect reader, based on the contents of their book. They follow up by providing consultancy services, in the area of their expertise, to delegates who need more in-depth help than they can gain from a week's training course or weekend workshop.

Turn your book into an information product

This is probably the easiest method. You first run a seminar, as above, and video it for home use on DVD. Then take the audio track from the video and produce a CD for use in the car. It doesn't require rocket science to produce a workbook for the seminar or workshop and publish it in the same style and colour as your book. All you need now is to box all this up, with your book, to make a home-study kit on your topic. You can then sell the home-study kit to your perfect reader through a one-page website. Simple!

Become a Keynote speaker

Assuming you're not one of those who would rather die than stand up and speak, it's very simple to take the underlying theme of your book and turn it into a 90-minute, keynote speech. You are a *published expert* now, so people will want to hear you speak on your topic. If you've followed my recommendations, you wrote your book from memory, without doing any research. Therefore, it will not be a great challenge for you to prepare a visual presentation from the key points in your book. You can then talk to networking groups or clubs full of your perfect readers. Of course, at the back of the room you will have signed copies of your book and your home-study kit for people to buy – at any price you choose to sell them.

How Effective is Self-promotion?

The simple solution for authors, who don't know where to promote their book, is to promote it EVERYWHERE! Here's a great example from one of my newly published 90-day authors.

'Looking forward to celebrating with you all at our Celebration Dinner on Sunday. I attended a ministerial event earlier in the week and all I did was tell some important person that I had just written a book and what the book was about. Now I've just been offered an opportunity to undertake a professional doctorate. The moral is, tell everyone you meet – whether they appear interested or not. You never know who they are or who they know. I'm getting this scary feeling that my book is going to open some doors. So I must get ready to handle what it brings with it! It felt right, from the word go. I can smell the aroma of sweet success.'

Ruth Tosin Oshikanlu,
RN (Adult), RM, RSCPHN (Health Visiting), QN, midwife, health visitor and author of: Tune In To Your Baby: Because babies don't come with an instruction manual, www.tuneintoyourbaby.co.uk

Will You Get Published?

All these strategies for promoting your book and your expertise assume that you will get your book published after you finish writing the manuscript. It's possible that a mainstream publisher will take it on. But, even if you follow the guidance in this book and first write a book proposal to avoid the seven costliest mistakes of unsuccessful authors, there's still no guarantee that you will get published by a traditional publishing house. And even if you do, it will still be you who needs to market it.

But what can you do you do if you can't get a publisher to take your book on?

Luckily, there are two other avenues open to you. You can self-publish, but that certainly isn't for the faint-hearted or those short of time. Alternatively, if you attend one of my seminars, you may qualify to join my 90-day mentoring programme. If so, my own publishing company would be happy to publish your book when you've finished writing it using my methods.

Now select the method of book promotion you will adopt and write it up as a marketing plan.

> Write the marketing plan for your book in the WHERE section of your Sure-fire Book Proposal Workbook at the end of this chapter or back of the book.

Summary

In this chapter, we've looked at secret number six – to know WHERE to promote your book.

You should now write some notes and pin them up where you can see them while you're writing your book.

Better still; complete the relevant sections of the Sure-fire Book Proposal Workbook at the end of this chapter or back of the book. As you complete each chapter and learn how to avoid each mistake, you will find that there's a section in the workbook for you to write down your answer. Then they will all be in one place for you to review before doing any writing.

If you'd prefer not to write in the book, you may download a copy of the workbook from:

www.TheSuccessfulAuthor.com/resources

Knowing the secrets of successful authors will help you to avoid the mistakes made by unsuccessful authors. But, clearly, we can't cover everything that you need to know and do within a book. That's why we run group workshops and a series of online webinars. These are designed to walk you through our Sure-fire Book Proposal process. They are designed to drill down into the essential details of your WHAT, WHO, WHY, HOW, WHEN, WHERE, WHICH and provide you with valuable feedback on how you can improve your proposal - and your book.

Remember, it's much faster and easier to refine a book proposal before you start writing your book than it is to rewrite your whole book after it's finished.

If you'd like to discover more about our webinars, workshops or coaching programmes, please visit:

www.TheSuccessfulAuthor.com

NOTES: Secret 6: WHERE to promote your book

Book marketing plan.

- ☐ Press Releases.
- ☐ Book Exhibitions.
- ☐ Media interviews – radio and TV.
- ☐ Getting influential reviewers to review it.
- ☐ Promotional video.
- ☐ Internet marketing.
- ☐ Social media.
- ☐ Product Launches.
- ☐ Conventional advertising in conventional media.

Details:

SECRET 7

WHICH SPECIALISTS TO USE

Secret number seven is to know exactly WHICH specialists to use. Going it alone is an all-too-familiar story and I'm not just talking about book writing.

You see, I'm a project manager and I know how to get things done. Yet, all through my career, I've come across people that inadvertently sabotage their opportunities for success. Sometimes they just don't know enough about what they're doing. Or if they do, they set off in the wrong direction because they skipped the basics. In other cases, people take on too much, or lose focus, and just can't finish what they started.

Becoming a published author is not rocket science. Aspiring authors just need to adhere to proven principles, and follow a few pre-defined steps, in order to get the right things done on time - the things they wanted to achieve and promised themselves that they would.

Writing a book is a superficially simple task. You just start on page one and write until you finish on the last page. Right?

If only it were that simple!

If you've already made a start on writing your book, then you'll already know what I mean. If you haven't, then you still have an opportunity to learn from this book and avoid the costliest mistakes.

Here is a list of the specialists I use to take my author's books from original idea into print. Which do you need?

- **Project managers**
- **Book mentors**
- **Book coaches**
- **Editors**
- **Proofreaders**
- **Illustrators**
- **Book designers**
- **Typesetters**
- **Cover designers**
- **Literary agents**
- **Publishers**
- **Book printers**
- **Book distributors**
- **Book promoters**
- **PR agents**
- **Website designers**

Make a note of the types of specialists you will need and write them in the WHICH section of your Sure-fire Book Proposal Workbook at the end of this chapter or back of the book.

It was no accident that I became a publisher and author's mentor. Twenty years as a corporate project manager planning and managing multi-million pound projects had taught me a lot about getting things done on time and to quality.

When I planned, wrote and published my own book in four weeks, people were surprised that it was even possible. Not me, because I didn't know it was supposed to take longer than that! Since then, I've learned that the average time to write a book is about 18 months, and that it can take a further 18 months for it to be published. And that's not counting the months of heartache trying to find a publisher that will accept your book proposal in the first place. Did I say book proposal? Isn't that what this book is about? Hmmm, that's interesting ...

Anyway, since I published my first book, I've developed a thriving business by helping others to do the same. I've subsequently published twenty-two books; each one planned, written, published and printed in less than 90 days. Some books were completed in even less than 20 days. During that time, the systematic-process and project-management techniques that I'd previously used to write and publish my first book were refined and simplified, so now anyone can do it.

'These days, even ordinary people can write a book and become an expert overnight. But they still need specialist help to actually do it!'

Helen Turier, RGN MAR
Resilience and Wellbeing Practitioner, trainer and author of four books: Bounce-back Ability, Get Back on Your Feet Again, Managing Pressure and Change Effectively, and Discover How Your Lifestyle Could be Killing You
www.helenturier.com

If you'd like some help, then join me and my team and spend a weekend getting your complete book proposal done – fast.

You may be surprised to discover that, to meet a particular business target, the first edition of the book you're reading now was designed, planned, written and then edited in a long weekend. Can you believe that? Then I got it published and printed so I could hold it in my hand just five days later. Why did I do it so quickly? Because I had a promotional opportunity that I couldn't resist and I already had a writing system that works, so I just did what I had to do to make it work even faster!

Of course, it wasn't perfect, but it fulfilled its strategic purpose for ten months. Now you're reading the second edition; that took another week!

Would you like to know how to get your book written more quickly than you expect – and then get on with your life – instead of spending between eighteen months and two years writing it and then waiting for a publisher?

Of course you would!

Why am I sharing all this with you? Well, I believe that *anyone* can write a book, using skills they already possess, if they follow a proven step-by-step system to get it published in weeks, not years.

So I set out to make the dream of becoming a published author a reality for anybody that wants it; this book was the first step towards making that happen.

However, over the years, I've come across coaches who make promises that they'll help people write their books - but they hide the fact that their success rates are abysmal. And that really annoys me. These people get many aspiring authors through the door, and then take the credit because a few naturally high-achieving writers became successful in spite of the hands-off style of coaching. What is worse, because their processes aren't based on sound project-management principles and proven mentoring techniques, they can't guarantee success. So many of their clients lose money and miss their opportunity to profit from being known as the 'expert' in their field.

Such a shame!

Because my programme has been adapted from proven processes and techniques, which I'd previously used as a project manager, results have been exceptional. In fact, I guarantee that *all* my clients will not only write a book, but will also hold it in their hands within 90 days of starting.

'Kevin, your ongoing 90-day mentoring programme (via the weekly group meetings, in combination with the one-to-one coaching) has really kept me on track and was absolutely essential. It worked a treat!

I am very impressed by your level of publishing success, and I would recommend (and have done so, several times) that anyone who is seriously considering writing and publishing a book look no further than your highly effective 90-day programme.'

Alun Richards
Website expert and author of two books, The Seven Critical Website Mistakes and Fire Your Webmaster
www.yourwebmasterisfired.co.uk

Four Reasons Book Projects Fail

1. Aspiring authors aren't motivated enough

For any book project to be successful, it needs a clear goal and purpose. Without dreams or goals, unsuccessful authors have no purpose or direction. They just don't know what they're doing or why. So this book was written to share my project-management experience and my insights into the problems of aspiring authors. Chapter 1 deals with this issue.

2. Aspiring authors procrastinate

For any book project to be successful, people need to take regular and timely action. It's not enough just to have good designs and the foolproof plans to implement them. If you don't take action, every day, then all is lost! Here are three of the reasons why people don't take action at the appropriate time - they all derive from fear of failure.

- **Limiting beliefs.** This issue is fully covered in my first book, *Change Your Limiting Beliefs*.

- **Insufficient benefits.** They believe the rewards from completing their book are too low. This issue is referred to in Chapter 1 (knowing your purpose for writing) and Chapter 6 (knowing where to promote it).

- **They don't know how.** This book is written to take aspiring authors through a step-by-step process, which ensures that they know exactly how to do everything needed to make progress with their book.

3. Aspiring authors get stuck

People get stuck on all sorts of projects and the following reasons are often the cause:

- **They get distracted.** They do research and include information they didn't already know and then get side-tracked - they may even decide to write a different book.

I always advise authors to write just what they already know about.

- **They have conflicting priorities.** For any project to be successful, it needs a clear goal and purpose. One of the benefits of this is that it's easy to manage priorities. Simply ask yourself: does this take me closer to, or further from, my goal? Your priority is now obvious.

- **They get overwhelmed** (too much to do). This is overcome by following a step-by-step process, where authors know exactly what and when they should be doing things. Tight focus is essential to avoid being distracted by other things that 'could' also be done. That's why a good plan, a rigid design, and a strong project manager are essential to keep accountability high and things moving.

4. Aspiring authors give up

- **It's too difficult.** They just don't know how to overcome problems that crop up. This book is written to take aspiring authors through a step-by-step process, which ensures that they know exactly how to do everything needed to complete their book.

- **They get demotivated.** Authors may feel that there are insufficient benefits in completing their book and become indecisive about continuing. This is related to Chapter 1 (knowing WHAT your purpose is in writing) and Chapter 6 (knowing WHERE to promote your book).

What Exactly is a Mentor's Job?

The key responsibilities of a mentor are:

- To manage the process of getting you finished on time (for example, within 90 days).

- To hold you accountable for delivering on your promises (for example, to require the timely delivery of each chapter).

- To help you to keep focused and on track (such as by providing group-training sessions and one-to-one coaching).

- To ask tough questions and push you for answers (to eliminate your excuses).

- To care about your success (but not enough to write your book for you!).

How Can Success be Guaranteed?

How can a coach or mentor guarantee that you'll complete your book successfully? Well, I've already mentioned the pedigree of the processes and techniques that we use ourselves; yet even they are not enough to guarantee success. You may find that out for yourself, as you work through this book.

Apart from a great design and planning processes, with proven techniques, there are three other things that aspiring authors need: three things that are essential.

'Writing this book has been an amazing experience. Not least, because I was a member of Kevin's fabulous Successful Author Academy. Full of brilliant people; each of whom succeeded in writing their own book within the same 90 days. Thank goodness for our Facebook group; those encouraging posts really kept me on track when I needed it most. The mutual support and encouragement provided by Kevin and the group really helped me to succeed.'

Helen Turier, RGN MAR
Resilience and Wellbeing Practitioner, trainer and author of four books:
Bounce-back Ability, Get Back on Your Feet Again, Managing Pressure and
Change Effectively, and Discover How Your Lifestyle Could be Killing You
www.helenturier.com

Firstly, you need a fully integrated system

You need to make sure that all the dots are already joined up! For example, we even have an online book-design tool that authors use to make the design of their book really easy – bullet-proof in fact - it even helps them manage their progress as they write their manuscript. Then they use an online project-management tool which helps to manage and administer their chapters' peer-review process. I can't tell you what a boon that is. SO look out for tools that can help you too.

Secondly, you need a proven plan

For my authors, I've actually prepared the foolproof writing plan myself. This ensures that they get off to a great start and complete their manuscript in either eight days or eight weeks, depending on which programme they choose. When their manuscript is completed and ready for editing, my a fully tested foolproof plan ensures that they get published and printed before the 90-day deadline is up. This all happens with very little input from authors. How can you do the same? Have you planned a successful project before that you could adapt?

Thirdly, you need support and management

There will always be times when the going gets tough and you lose heart. This is where an author's coach or mentor can make all the difference.

'Kevin coaches and mentors you as you write, providing a complete service that's truly amazing. In my case, after starting off really well, I found myself facing several major technical and domestic challenges along the way. But Kevin's positive approach, support, and guidance ensured I still finished what I'd started, and all within the 90 days. I can highly recommend his coaching and mentoring; his programmes are first class.'

Martin Cornes
Author of three books: The Ultimate Profit System, The Seven Killer Business Mistakes and Why Personal Development Doesn't Work
www.theultimateprofitsystem.co.uk

For example, we manage the complete writing process for authors and we literally 'hold their hand' as they write their manuscript.

It's an intense programme, because research shows that people lose focus if things take too long, so we make sure that everything is done on time, every time. I already know where in the programme authors will stumble, so I've made sure that we have built-in safety nets to catch you and get you back on track again.

Who do you know that could do that for you?

'Without Kevin Bermingham, my publisher, this book would not have happened! Everyone says that about their publisher, but I mean it. Kevin's sterling efforts of encouragement, support, sometimes cracking of the whip, and not forgetting his dry sense of humour, have kept me on track. Kevin has created a fine-tuned strategy that takes the hard work out of writing a book for all would-be authors. It takes dedication and commitment from the author and with Kevin's foolproof plan to follow; you're well on the road to success, while keeping your sanity!'

Elaine Noble,
Certified life coach and author of Everyday Mistakes That Undermine Your Confidence www.mistakesthatundermineyourconfidence.co.uk

Before someone follows one of my mentoring programmes, they will have been assessed to make sure that they have a good reason for writing their book. That gives our author's mentors the inside knowledge to make sure we can maintain their motivation at peak levels. Who will you get to do that?

Summary

In this chapter, we've looked at secret number seven - to know WHICH specialists to use.

You should now write some notes and pin them up where you can see them while you're writing your book.

Better still; complete the relevant sections of the Sure-fire Book Proposal Workbook at the end of this chapter or back of the book. As you complete each chapter and learn how to avoid each mistake, you will find that there's a section in the workbook for you to write down your answer. Then they will all be in one place for you to review before doing any writing.

If you'd prefer not to write in the book, you may download a copy of the workbook from:

www.TheSuccessfulAuthor.com/resources

Knowing the secrets of successful authors will help you to avoid the mistakes made by unsuccessful authors. But, clearly, we can't cover everything that you need to know and do within a book. That's why we run group workshops and a series of online webinars. These are designed to walk you through our Sure-fire Book Proposal process. They are designed to drill down into the essential details of your WHAT, WHO, WHY, HOW, WHEN, WHERE, WHICH and provide you with valuable feedback on how you can improve your proposal - and your book.

Remember, it's much faster and easier to refine a book proposal before you start writing your book than it is to rewrite your whole book after it's finished.

If you'd like to discover more about our webinars, workshops or coaching programmes, please visit:

www.TheSuccessfulAuthor.com

NOTES: Secret 7: WHICH specialists to use

Which types of specialists will you need?

- ☐   Project managers.
- ☐   Book mentors.
- ☐   Book coaches.
- ☐   Editors.
- ☐   Proofreaders.
- ☐   Illustrators.
- ☐   Book designers.
- ☐   Typesetters.
- ☐   Cover designers.
- ☐   Literary agents.
- ☐   Publishers.
- ☐   Book printers.
- ☐   Book distributors.
- ☐   Book promoters.
- ☐   PR agents.
- ☐   Website designers.

NEXT STEPS

I congratulate you on getting this far. It tells me that you're determined to make a success of your book and avoid the mistakes that I see so many aspiring authors making.

Kevin Bermingham

Thishis book was written to help you to avoid the mistakes made by unsuccessful authors. I help aspiring authors to discover those secrets by first getting them to write a book proposal, before starting to write their book.

By now, you should have an outline sketch of a book proposal and I can promise that you will find it a great help to you when you're writing your book. But if you want to take your book to the next level, then you'll really need to master the subtleties.

You see, the more time spent planning and designing your book up front, the faster it will be completed; you are less likely to get stuck along the way or to need major rewrites after your book is written.

Along with your first chapter, a book proposal is something that you can confidently send to a literary agent or publisher (you'll also need a one-page summary). Of course, I can't guarantee success in getting a publishing contract; that's down to you and your topic. But as a publisher myself, I would value an author's well-considered book proposal.

Remember, it's much faster and easier to refine your book proposal and its subsequent book design before you start writing your book, than it is to correct or rewrite your book after it's written!

Clearly, we haven't covered everything that you will need to know to write an effective book proposal. That's why we walk you through our Sure-fire Book Proposal process during our regular webinars and workshops.

These are designed to drill down into the essential details of your **WHAT, WHO, WHY, HOW, WHEN, WHERE** questions.

You will also get some valuable feedback on how you can improve your book. We may even suggest improvements in ways that you hadn't even considered.

'Words cannot express my appreciation and indebtedness to Kevin Bermingham, book coach, editor and publisher. He is an inspiration and his enthusiasm for his '90-day book' project was infectious; I had to 'get writing'. There is a book in each and every one of us.'

Lynn Tulip Chartered MCIPD
Independent career consultant, counsellor and HR professional.
Author of two books: Get That Job: The art of successful job hunting and Can't Get That Job: Seven killer CV mistakes that destroy your chances of job success
www.getthatjobbook.com

Our workshop really isn't designed for everyone. It's certainly NOT for 'no-hopers', looking to 'give it a go'.

- It's NOT for the sort of person who's used to saying, 'if only'.

- It's NOT for people aren't committed to their own success.

- It's NOT for dreamers who can't commit to action.

- It's NOT for people who find it hard to work to tight deadlines.

- It's DEFINITELY NOT for people who talk big, but never deliver anything tangible.

The **SUCCESSFUL** AUTHOR *Academy Programme*

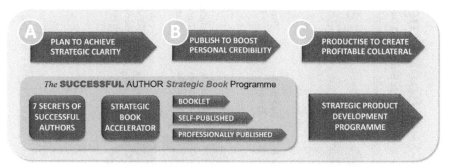

The workshop is part of our academy programme and is designed to fast-track committed individuals: people with experience of life who have expertise in their own field, who want to write books that will make a difference.

- It is FOR people who are prepared to commit to a better future and to strive for success.

- It is FOR people who welcome an intensive and demanding challenge.

- It is FOR people who aspire to invest just 90 minutes a day, for the next eight weeks.

- It is FOR people who are prepared to be eased out of their comfort zones to get the results they deserve.

The Successful Author 90-Day Book Programme

A Guaranteed System for WRITING & PUBLISHING a Strategic Book in 90 Days, or Less

1.Propose	2.Prototype	3.Plan	4. Produce	5.Prepare	6.Publish	7.Promote™
			Cover & Copy Edit	Design & Typeset™	Promotion Pack	Completion Kit Delivery
1. Sure-Fire Strategy	Chapter Three	Chapter Four	Consolidate & Proofread	Publish Amazon & Kindle	Celebration Dinner & Awards	
2. Bullet-Proof Outline	Chapter Two	Chapter Five	Chapter Seven +	Print & Dispatch	DAY-90 Book Delivered	
3.Fool-Proof Writing Plan	Chapter One +	Chapter Six				

THE SUCCESSFUL AUTHOR

COACHING & ACCOUNTABILITY

The 90-Day Programme Contains Just Eight Weeks of Writing

SUCCESSFUL

AUTHORS SHARE THEIR OWN SECRETS

Helen Turier

**Author of *Bounce-back Ability*
and three other books.**

MY SECRET 'This book would still be in the planning stages if Kevin Bermingham hadn't taken me through his 90-Day Book Programme. Writing this book has been an amazing experience. Not least, because I was a member of his fabulous Successful Author Academy. Full of brilliant people; each of whom succeeded in writing their own book within the same 90 days. Thank goodness for our Facebook group; those encouraging posts really kept me on track when I needed it most. The mutual support and encouragement provided by Kevin and the group really helped me to succeed.'

DISCOVER HOW YOUR **LIFESTYLE COULD BE KILLING YOU**

CREATING ULTIMATE WELLBEING™ USING THE B.O.U.N.C.E.™ MODEL OF RESILIENCE

Helen

Martin Cornes

Author of *The Ultimate Profit System* and two others.

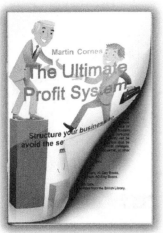

MY SECRET 'Kevin coaches and mentors you; providing a complete service that's truly amazing. In my case, after starting off really well, I found myself facing several major technical and domestic challenges along the way. But Kevin's positive approach, support, and guidance ensured I still finished what I'd started, and all within the 90 days. I can highly recommend this first-class programme. It easily proves the truth that "We've all got a book within us".'

Lynn Tulip

Author of *Get That Job* and *Can't Get That Job*.

MY SECRET 'If anyone had asked me if I could write a book 90 days ago, the answer would have been questionable. I never believed I could, but I have! The amazing feeling of holding my completed book within 90 days – and then selling it – is something special to experience. Thank you Kevin, book coach and publisher; your inspiration and encouragement have been awesome. I'd recommend you and your 90-day programme to anyone – because we all have a book in us!'

Get That Job
The art of successful job hunting

Elaine Noble

Author of *Everyday Mistakes That Undermine Your Confidence.*

Everyday Mistakes
That Undermine
Your Confidence

Discover How You Unwittingly Sabotage
Your Opportunities To Get Ahead In Life

Elaine Noble

MY SECRET 'Without someone like Kevin Bermingham, this book would not have happened! Everyone says that about their publisher, but I mean it. Kevin's sterling efforts of encouragement, support, sometimes cracking of the whip, and not forgetting his dry sense of humour, have kept me on track. Kevin has created a fine-tuned strategy that takes the hard work out of writing a book for all would-be authors. It takes dedication and commitment from the author and with Kevin's foolproof plan to follow you're well on the road to success, while keeping your sanity!'

Jennie Harland-Khan

Author of *I'm Back.*

MY SECRET 'Kevin kicked my butt and gave me the push I needed to write a book in ninety days. Kevin's promise of structure, hand-holding, simplicity and, above all, a 90-day deadline was what made me take the plunge and sign up. He didn't disappoint me. The whole process was painless and all my overwhelm was eliminated because I got to focus on just one chapter at a time. Apart from Kevin's personal encouragement, what made him stand out from other mentors I've had in the past was his RELENTLESS desire to ensure I succeeded. The result: my first book was published within 90 days – start to finish. Awesome!'

SURE-FIRE

BOOK PROPOSAL WORKBOOK

 **H**ere is where you can put all of the work you have done on the seven secrets together into a Sure-fire Book Proposal Workbook. Doing this will help you to avoid the seven costliest mistakes that all unsuccessful authors make.

Use this Workbook to consolidate all of the answers you gave to the seven questions, or just to tidy up the answers you gave at the end of each chapter.

Of course, your book proposal should be completed in its entirety *before* **you attempt to start writing your book.**

The Sure-fire Book Proposal Workbook is also available to download if you don't want to write in this book. Get it from:

www.theSuccessfulAuthor.com/resources

Sure-Fire Book Proposal Workbook

AUTHOR'S NAME..

MOBILE NUMBER ....

Why write a book?

- ❑ Make a profit.
- ❑ Leave a legacy.
- ❑ Increase your credibility.
- ❑ Support your business.
- ❑ Win more clients.
- ❑ Clarify and focus your thoughts.

Think about YOUR own very specific reason. Now, make a note below of WHY your book is important to you.

1. What **WILL** happen if you **DON'T** write your book?

2. What **WILL NOT** happen if you **DON'T** write your book?

3. What **WILL** happen if you **DO** write your book?

4. What **WILL NOT** happen if you **DO** write your book?

The SEVEN SECRETS of Successful Authors

A Proven System for PLANNING a Strategic Book That Avoids Costly Mistakes and Creates More Profit!

1. What?

WHAT to Write About

MOTIVATING TOPIC

LEARN ABOUT:
- Motivating Book Topic:
  - Problems
  - Passions
  - Proficiencies
- Book Title
- Subtitles

2. Who?

WHO to Write For

PERFECT READER

LEARN ABOUT:
- Choosing For Whom to Write
- Demographic Profiles
- Perfect Reader:
  - Names
  - Situations
  - Challenges
  - Objections
  - Attitudes
  - Real Quotes
  - Inside Story

3. Why?

WHY Readers Buy Books

YOUR BOOK'S PROMISE

LEARN ABOUT:
- Psychographic Profiles
- Reader's Problems
- Author's Solutions
- Compelling Sales Copy
- Main Themes
- Your Book's Promise

4. How?

HOW to Design Book

BULLET-PROOF DESIGN

LEARN ABOUT:
- The 3-Book Design Strategy
- Book Title
- Book Design Disciplines
- Book Design Software
- Chapter Heads
- Sections Heads
- Subsections
- Cover Design Specification
- Marketing Blurb Design
- Author Bio.

5. When?

WHEN to Finish Writing

FOOL-PROOF WRITING PLAN

LEARN ABOUT:
- Cyclic Writing Strategy
- Book Management Software
- Author's Work Schedule (Write, Edit & Review)
- Publisher's Work Schedule (Design, Edit & Publishing)
- Print & Delivery Schedule

6. Where?

WHERE to Promote Book

MARKETING PLAN

LEARN ABOUT:
- People
- Place
- Price
- Promotion:
  - Brochure
  - Flyer
  - Networking
  - Website
  - Download
  - Articles
  - Blog Posts
  - Videos
  - Seminars
  - Workshops
  - Workbooks

7. Which?

WHICH Specialists

SUPPORT PLAN

LEARN ABOUT:
- Step-by-Step Programmes
- Defined Set of Deliverables
- List of Technical Specialists
- Coach/Mentors
- Project Managers
- Accountability
- Peer Support
- Communities
- Guaranteed Results

© 2013 K.Bermingham

THE SUCCESSFUL AUTHOR
www.TheSuccessfulAuthor.com

Secret 1: WHAT to write about

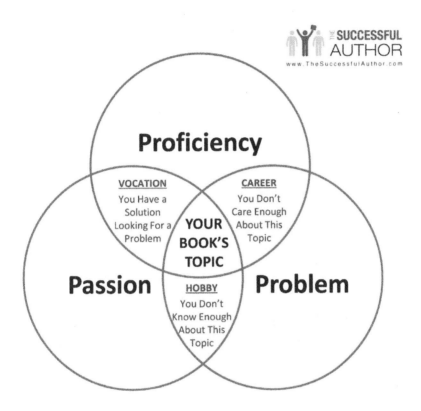

Book topic

What **Problem** do you want to solve?

What's the one problem that you feel strongly about?

What's Your **Passion**?

What do you love that you'd miss if you had to give it up?

What's Your **Proficiency**?

What's easy for you, but friends always ask for help with?

Turn these words or statements into a sentence, as follows.

I want to use my passion for

....

and my proficiency in

....

to

....

the problem of

....

So, My TOPIC is

....

My topic-related book title is:

Now use one of the following beginnings to write a paragraph as your author's personal statement
(Maximum of 70 words).

"I believe that...."
"I think..."
"What really annoys me is..."

Secret 2: WHO to write for

Type of reader

Reader's demographic profile.

Reader's psychographic profile.

Ideal reader

Reader's name(s) (Attach their photograph later).

Reader's situation (Life, how do they feel about it?).

Reader's problems and challenges.

1.

2.

3.

Reader's objections to solving these problems.

- ☐ Insufficient time.
- ☐ Lack of money.
- ☐ I don't believe it will work.
- ☐ I don't believe it will work for me.
- ☐ I don't trust you.
- ☐ I don't need it.

Make a list of your answers to each of those objections.

Reader's attitude to your book's topic.

Sample of quotations made by your readers.
What they've said about their life.

Reader's Story.
Get into rapport, then record it.

Secret 3: WHY your readers buy books

Reader's one big problem.
That keeps them awake at night.

What's the key question they would ask you if they could?

What do they need to know?

Promise

Your answer to your reader's key question.
This is your key message.

```
┌─────────────────────────────────────────────┐
│                                             │
│                                             │
│                                             │
│                                             │
└─────────────────────────────────────────────┘
```

Write down six or seven supporting messages.

1.

2.

3.

4.

5.

6.

7

What is your book's promise?

Book's main theme (Based on your promise).

Feasible selling price of your book (Check on Amazon).

Secret 4: HOW to design your book

Book Structure
Category of book.

Type of book.

Internal structure type.

Final book title.
To attract attention. (Less than 8 words).

Subtitle.
Explains what it's about. (Less than 16 words).

Cover design elements.

Contents list:

[Title Page]

[Copyright page]

Author's other books (optional).

Dedication/Acknowledgements (optional).

Introduction (optional).

Chapter titles.

1.

2.

3.

4.

5.

6.

7.

Conclusion.

Next steps (Your sales pitch).

About the author and author's personal statement.

Book Cover

Book Title.

To attract attention. (Less than 8 words)

Subtitle.

Explains what it's about. (Less than 16 words)

Rear Heading.

Why should I buy this book? Could be Reader's key Question, or your Promise.

(Less than 16 words)

Rear Blurb.

Why should I buy this book now? Your Key Messages; the Benefits of reading it; could include a testimonial.

(Less than 150 words total)

Author's biography and photo.

Why should I listen to you? (Less than 50 words total)

Secret 5: WHEN to finish writing

Writing strategy.

Overall start and end date.

Chapter start and end dates.
Introduction

1.

2.

3.

4.

5.

6.

7.

Conclusion

Quality criteria.

Performance criteria.

Secret 6: WHERE to promote your book

Book marketing plan

- ☐ Press Releases.
- ☐ Book Exhibitions.
- ☐ Media interviews – radio and TV.
- ☐ Getting influential reviewers to review it.
- ☐ Promotional video.
- ☐ Internet marketing.
- ☐ Social media.
- ☐ Product Launches.
- ☐ Conventional advertising in conventional media.

Details:

Secret 7: WHICH specialists to use

Which types of specialists will you need?

- ☐ Project managers.
- ☐ Book mentors.
- ☐ Book coaches.
- ☐ Editors.
- ☐ Proofreaders.
- ☐ Illustrators.
- ☐ Book designers.
- ☐ Typesetters.
- ☐ Cover designers.
- ☐ Literary agents.
- ☐ Publishers.
- ☐ Book printers.
- ☐ Book distributors.
- ☐ Book promoters.
- ☐ PR agents.
- ☐ Website designers.

If you'd prefer not to write in this book, you may
download a copy of the workbook from:

www.TheSuccessfulAuthor.com/resources

Follow the link below to discover more about author's workshops,
webinars and coaching programmes.

www.TheSuccessfulAuthor.com

ABOUT
THE AUTHOR

Kevin Bermingham

MBA, BSc, DipM, CMC, MPracNLP

Author, mentor, book publisher,
Certified Project Management Consultant.

I n the past, I've planned and managed multi-million-pound projects for several large corporations, such as the Civil Aviation Authority, National Air-Traffic Services, London Electricity, SEEBOARD and Nokia. I've been 'getting things done' successfully for more than 20 years and I'm proud of the fact that I've already helped over 1,000 people to achieve their goals and have many glowing testimonials.

As a project manager, I frequently overcame problems using a set of simple project-management techniques, which were applicable to any situation, for example the setting of very tight deadlines. You see, research shows that our ability to achieve goals quickly drops off after just 90 days[12].

So, in 2010, I wrote and published my first book, *Change Your Limiting Beliefs*, using these same simple techniques – and I did it in just 30 days ... because I didn't know it was supposed to take longer than that!

Then, in 2012, I used the same techniques to take my first group of aspiring authors from Proposal, through Prototyping, Planning, Producing, Preparation, Publishing, and then into Productising, Packaging and Promotion – all within 90 days! At the same time, I built my own Successful Author Academy and publishing business from scratch within just 90 days.

I now run one-to-one, bespoke mentoring programmes for business-owners, entrepreneurs and specialists, plus fully integrated group-mentoring and publishing programmes.

---

12   Matta, N. F. and Ashkenas, R. N., 'Why good projects fail anyway', Harvard Business Review, Sep 2003, Volume: 81 Issue: 9 pp.109-114

> I work with business-owners, entrepreneurs and specialists.

I have worked with many business-owners, entrepreneurs and specialists who aspired to become successful authors in their fields of expertise. They're people who wanted to increase their credibility FAST and stand head and shoulders above their competitors. They all used the following ABC formula to write a **Strategic Book**.

- **Achieve Strategic Clarity.** Planning a clear strategic direction gives focus.

- **Boost Personal Credibility.** Publishing a Strategic Book enhances your personal reputation.

- **Create Profitable Collateral.** Productising creates profit from your existing skills and knowledge and that collateral creates pre-sold prospects who want to become customers.

In 2012, I wrote the first edition of *The Seven Secrets of Successful Authors,* so that aspiring authors would have a better chance of writing a Strategic Book quickly and then getting it published - by writing the Right Book!

The Successful Author Academy combines workshops, group mentoring and one-to-one coaching to convert the skills, knowledge and expertise that people already have into a professionally published book within just 90 days. We also put each book onto Amazon and Kindle. Our programmes all use simple project-management techniques that achieve guaranteed results. Aspiring authors follow a rigid, step-by-step weekly programme, so that they always know exactly what, when and how to do whatever's needed. We allow no discretion or flexibility to deviate from either the design or the plan they created. If they don't follow their plan, they get 'fired'. Most people need that level of motivation.

We've all heard people who say, 'I'd like to write a book' or 'I've got a book inside me', yet somehow we never see anything in print. Maybe you know someone like that?

I'm known for helping business-owners, entrepreneurs and specialists to write a Strategic Book that gives them more clarity, credibility and collateral than their competitors.

My mission is to get the Right Book out of your head and into your hands FAST, so you can quickly get on with your life.

Kevin Bermingham

Author, mentor, book publisher,
Certified Project Management Consultant.
www.KevinBermingham.com

Lightning Source UK Ltd.
Milton Keynes UK
UKOW06f1219300114

225559UK00001B/20/P